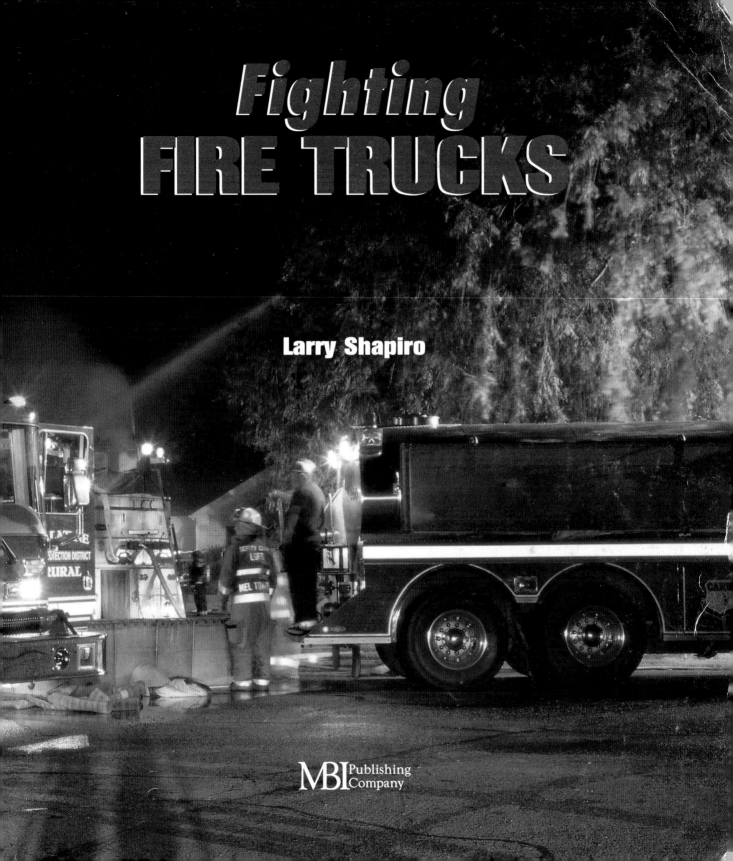

Fighting
FIRE TRUCKS

Larry Shapiro

MBI Publishing Company

First published in 1999 by MBI Publishing Company, 729 Prospect Avenue, PO Box 1, Osceola, WI 54020-0001 USA

The information in this book is true and complete to the best of our knowledge. All recommendations are made without any guarantee on the part of the author or Publisher, who also disclaim any liability incurred in connection with the use of this data or specific details.

We recognize that some words, model names and designations, for example, mentioned herein are the property of the trademark holder. We use them for identification purposes only. This is not an official publication.

MBI Publishing Company books are also available at discounts in bulk quantity for industrial or sales-promotional use. For details write to Special Sales Manager at Motorbooks International Wholesalers & Distributors, 729 Prospect Avenue, Osceola, WI 54020-0001 USA.

Designed by Rebecca Allen
Edited by Sara Nelson
Printed in Hong Kong

Library of Congress Cataloging-in-Publication Data

Shapiro, Larry.
    Fighting fire trucks/Larry Shapiro.
        p. cm. --(Enthusiast color series)
    Includes index.
    ISBN 0-7603-0595-1 (pbk.: alk. paper)
    1. Fire engines. 2. Fire extinction. I. Title. II. Series.
TH9371.S46   1999
628.9'25--dc21   98-50757

On the front cover: The Progress Hose Company of Harrisburg, Pennsylvania, uses its brand-new Seagrave custom pumper. The canopy over the hosebed is fashioned after a design used by the FDNY. The cab has seating for 10 firefighters.

On the frontispiece: Rosemont, Illinois' 95-foot E-One tower ladder is one of six elevated master streams that went to work at an abandoned lumberyard fire that required five alarms.

On the title page: Although the bulk of the fire has been knocked down, two tankers stand by to dump water to ensure there is an adequate supply for hitting the remaining hot spots.

On the back cover: A forward lay puts the Pierce engine right in front of the house, allowing firefighters to pull the pre-connects to attack the fire. Unfortunately, this fire had a head start and required a defensive attack.

CONTENTS

ACKNOWLEDGMENTS

Every author, in an attempt to acknowledge those who served as an inspiration, resource, or contributor in some way, will inadvertently overlook someone. To those of you who find yourself in this position, I apologize now. Many people took time out of their busy lives to answer my questions, and then explained things again to me more slowly when I didn't quite get everything the first time. I wish to thank them, and those who have helped me either gain access to the fire ground to create these images, or who have worked with me over the years so that I can continually photograph exciting new rigs.

There have been some important individuals in my life (not listed below) who have been patient and understanding through my adventures with the fire service. Never once has there been a discouraging word when I, as the driver, have made an unexpected detour after hearing something broadcast over the fire frequencies, or when I saw a nice header in the sky. (Most of this is, of course, said tongue-in-cheek.) I am referring to my wife, Dorothy, who has in the past been heard referring to the occasional fire image as beautiful, and my oldest boys James and Paul, who for the most part would be content never laying eyes on a fire truck again. My biggest hope is for Scott, my youngest, who has accompanied me on numerous visits to fire stations, truck shoots, working fires, and a national trade show where he proceeded to ignore my instructions and get lost among 100 or so display rigs as they all started their engines to drive out of the Hoosier Dome in Indianapolis. My father once told me that the best wish he could have for me would be to have a son just like me.

With that said, the following people, listed alphabetically, are due my utmost gratitude: Jim Bodony, Mid-America Truck and Equipment Co.; District Chief Dan Bonkowski, Northbrook, IL; Fire Chief Ron Colpaert, Winnetka, IL; Jack Connors; Roger Coulter, GFE, Inc.; Lieut. Ben Donovan, Lutherville, MD VFD; Lieut. Joe Downey, FDNY Rescue 2; J.T. Duke, Fire & Rescue Apparatus; Fire Chief Steve Dumovich, Wilmette, IL; Assistant Chief Doug Edwards, Cherry Valley FPD, IL; Jim Eggleston, FWD Seagrave Co.; Deputy District Chief Eddie Enright, Chicago, IL; Captain John Ferry and the members of FDNY Rescue 5; Fire Chief Tom Freeman, Lisle-Woodridge Fire District, IL; Fire Chief Ron Gould, Prospect Heights FPD, IL; Deputy Chief Ed Haase, Prospect Heights FPD, IL; Rob Haldeman, LTI, Inc.;

An engine company gets ready to put a master stream into service as fire vents itself through a truss-roof grocery store in Wheeling, Illinois.

George Hall; Lieut. Harvey Harrell, FDNY Rescue 5; Chief Don Heinbuch, Baltimore City Fire Department; District Chief Norm Johnson, Glenview, IL; Mike King, Specialty Vehicle Service; retired engineer Sully Kolomay, Chicago Fire Department, Engine Co. 98; Deputy Chief Chuck Kramer, Arlington Heights, IL; Ken Lenz, HME, Inc.; District Chief David Lozeau, Chicago, IL; FF Tom McDonald, FDNY Technical Services Division; Larry McGloughlin; Battalion Chief Bob McKee, Chicago, IL; Tony Mastrobattista, LTI, Inc.; Robert Meade, Airport Training Officer, O'Hare International Airport; Commander Michael Milkes, Glencoe, IL; Roger Parker, Luverne Fire Apparatus; Glen Prezembel, Mid-America Truck and Equipment Co.; Fire Chief Jay Riordan, Northbrook, IL; Fire Chief Bruce Rodewald, Arlington Heights, IL; Captain Phil Ruvolo and the members of FDNY Rescue 2; Deputy Chief Tim Sashko, Buffalo Grove, IL; John Schafer, The Sutphen Corporation; District Chief Drew Smith, Prospect Heights FPD, IL; Deputy Chief Jerry Tonne, Lombard, IL; Bureau Chief Tony Vavra, Lisle-Woodridge Fire District, IL; FF Ken Wagner, FDNY Technical Services Division; Thomas Wagner, Airport Training Officer, O'Hare International Airport; Barbara Weber, Pierce Manufacturing; FF Tim Wellington, Winnetka, IL: Deputy Chief John Wente, Palatine, IL; Deputy Chief Craig Wilt, Cherry Valley FPD, IL; and Bob Winton, Win-Son, Inc.

Without trying to sound like an award recipient at the Academy Awards, I would be remiss if I didn't acknowledge my parents and siblings, who put up with the same lack of courtesy and compassion as my wife and children. Through high school, family vacations, and holidays, anytime a rig went by with a siren wailing, we made a detour. Years ago, before leaving for the airport in Boston, I asked the concierge at a hotel for the location of the nearest fire station. Priding himself on having an answer for everything readily at his fingertips, I stumped him with this one. After receiving the location, my parents sat in a taxicab as the firemen pulled the rigs out for pictures.

My wife, Dorothy, who serves as my editor, has finally gotten used to me getting up in the middle of the night to pursue my passions. She can rest assured, confident that my passions involve fires. This must be love.

INTRODUCTION

Fire trucks have always been fascinating for adults and children alike. In writing this book, I chose to rely on the knowledge and expertise of many individuals who have dedicated their lives to the fire service. Whether currently active or retired, these men spent time with me sharing stories, experiences, and training to help produce a book that would include the duties associated with different types of fire apparatus instead of relying solely on the physical attributes of the vehicles. In doing so, we have come up with a book that has exciting photographs of each type of fire apparatus, and offers the reader a bit of knowledge about the work that is being done in the images shown, and every day throughout the country.

The fire service commands loyalty unlike any other profession. Countless men and women can be found following in the footsteps of their parents, grandparents, and siblings to carry on the proud traditions that make up this exciting field.

Statistically, total annual fires in the United States are down, but injuries to civilians and fire-fighters, along with fatalities, are up. In 1996, there were 4,500 civilian fire deaths; the number increased in 1997 to 4,900. At the same time, 1997 was the first year the number of fires was less than 2 million. The United States leads the free world in the number of fire codes, fire deaths, injuries related to fires, and the total dollar loss resulting from fires. One can only hope that increased public education and compliance with codes and laws will help to reduce the number of fires, while at the same time preserve lives.

This is not meant as a textbook for instructional purposes, but simply as a means to assist all of the "armchair" fire chiefs who have never had the opportunity of manning a handline or conducting a search through a smoke-filled building for a trapped occupant. For those of you who are currently working in the fire service (or have in the past) and have experienced this excitement, you have both my jealousy and my utmost respect and admiration.

CHAPTER 1

PUMPERS

Thick smoke was venting from the eaves around the roof of the commercial storefront as first-due Engine 27 arrived on the scene. Pre-connects were pulled and the engineer used a forward lay to make the hydrant, which was right out front. The officer didn't need much of a size-up to make an immediate call for extra alarms as the company went to work attempting entry into the fire building. The intense heat and fire prevented the companies from making an interior attack.

This four-alarm blaze in a shopping center required a response from 15 engine companies and four trucks. The E-One engine draws its water supply through a front intake. The firefighters with the nonstandard silver suits responded from a nearby military air base.

The most common type of fire engine in departments throughout the United States is the pumper. Terminology can vary between the names pumper and engine, which mean the same thing. This is a unit that carries water and has a pump, hose, and ladders. It is <u>not</u> a fire *truck*. In the fire service, "truck" refers to a vehicle with a permanently mounted aerial device (see chapter 2). Pumpers come in many sizes and shapes and can be painted virtually any color or design. When referring to the unit and the personnel that accompany it, the proper term is *engine company*.

Paraphrasing the National Fire Protection Association (NFPA), a pumper is defined as a unit carrying at least 500 gallons of water with the capacity to pump 750 or more gallons per minute. In addition, it must also have at least 48 feet of ground ladders plus a minimum of 1,600 feet of fire hose for attack and supply.

A pumper uses a truck chassis, which can be purchased from commercial truck manufacturers such as Ford, GMC, Freightliner, International Harvester (IHC), and Peterbilt. Many chassis are designed specifically for the fire service and are built by special chassis companies or businesses that fabricate the entire pumper. Custom chassis manufacturers have included HME, Spartan, Duplex, and Pemfab although, as of this writing, only HME and Spartan

Like many large cities, Chicago utilizes the reverse lay for its engines. Here, Engine 5 supplies several lines at a 5-11 alarm fire. For many years, Chicago purchased pumpers utilizing commercial Ford C-Series chassis with bodies by E-One.

Left
Chicago Engine 89 uses its master stream to hit hot spots at a 5-11 alarm fire in a block-long building. In the background, several other master streams are visible. The 5-11 designation dates back to the days before radios when the Joker Stand tapped out all information like a ticker tape. The alarm level followed by the number 11 on the tape designated extra alarms.

Right
Positioned in front of the fire building, this pumper supplies water to a Snorkel, and provides light for the front of the building using several telescoping 500-watt quartz lights.

Firefighters in suburban Pittsburgh battled a house fire on top of a hill. All of the handlines and equipment had to be walked up the long driveway, which would not accommodate a full-size pumper.

remain in the industry. Others that build complete apparatus include Pierce, Emergency One (E-One), Seagrave, Sutphen, and Kovatch Mobile Equipment Company (KME). Complete builders no longer in the industry are American LaFrance, Mack, Grumman, Pirsch, Ward LaFrance, Crown, and Maxim, although the Freightliner Corporation has purchased the American LaFrance name and is bringing

A firefighter with full protective gear prepares to make entry into a well-involved structure during a training exercise. He is fully encapsulated with a Nomex hood, helmet, regulator, and 30-minute air bottle strapped to his back. On his belt is a motion-sensitive alarm that rings a loud piercing sound if the firefighter remains inactive for a prolonged period of time. This is a safeguard in the event that a firefighter becomes injured, rendering him unconscious. The alarm alerts other company members to his position.

it back into the fire service. Innovations available from the chassis companies, such as Anti-Lock Brake Systems, rear axles that steer like front axles, and tight 45-degree cramp angles for turning, have increased the options available to fire departments.

In addition to the chassis, the pumper also contains a fire pump mounted to the frame rails, a water tank, and a fabricated body made of a polynomer, aluminum, stainless steel, or galvaneal steel. Pumpers can seat as few as 4 people, or as many as 10 if supplied with an extended cab. The large extended cabs allow fire departments to customize the seating layouts, which include providing space for extra compartments, an inside operator's panel for the fire pump, or a command center for the chief.

Many departments need to be concerned about the overall size of the pumper due to their response

15

A Mack and an E-One pumper are on the scene of a boatyard fire on Long Island. Visible in the foreground is a large-diameter supply attached to a gated "Y" adapter that permits up to three smaller attack lines to run from this supply line.

districts. Older cities with smaller streets, lots of parked cars, and alleys require pumpers with a shorter wheelbase and a tighter turning radius. Since most commercial chassis are built with the engine ahead of the driver, these are likely to be longer than a custom chassis where the cab is over the engine.

The body of the pumper contains compartments for equipment storage. These can be arranged according to the manufacturer's standard layout, or they can be individualized to accommodate the specific items carried by each department. The compartment doors can hinge sideways, from the top, or they may roll up and not protrude from the vehicle when open. In any case, equipment placement is crucial for efficient operation at the scene of an emergency.

Some pumpers are set up to intake water from each of the four sides of the unit. Others are only designed with side intakes. This varies with the standard operating procedures (SOPs) of each department.

Hoses are connected to the pump to flow water through the discharges. Discharges can also be located on any of the four sides of the pumper.

Basic equipment carried on a pumper includes axes, pike poles, fire extinguishers, hand tools, an assortment of nozzles for the attack lines, self-contained breathing apparatus (SCBA), and fans for clearing smoke. Some departments carry sprinkler heads for automatic sprinkler systems. Whenever a fire suppression sprinkler system is activated, each head that opens up and flows water needs to be replaced.

Duties

The primary function of an engine company has always been to extinguish fires. Although this is still the case today, an engine company's duties also include responding to motor vehicle accidents, rescues, and any emergency that prompts someone to dial 911. In recent years, another responsibility has been added, which in many cases has become the primary duty for some engine companies. Under the heading of Emergency Medical Services (EMS), engine companies have become first responders to assist with the growing number of emergency medical requests. Dispatched in addition to an ambulance or medic unit, the engine company assists with manpower or begins medical treatment if they arrive first. Since the number of fires nationally has declined in the past decade, firefighters are trained to handle medical calls with basic first aid training, Emergency Medical Technician (EMT) training, or as full paramedics, in addition to their training in firefighting.

A certain amount of medical supplies is also part of the equipment complement on each pumper. Depending on the level of trained personnel on board, pumpers may be stocked with basic life support (BLS)

One of Philadelphia's engines works at a job in a row house.

or advanced life support (ALS) equipment. As a matter of fact, an ALS-equipped pumper has all the capabilities of an ALS ambulance without the means to transport a patient. Drugs, telemetry, and a defibrillator are part of an ALS engine that is staffed by

A custom pumper made by the Pirsch company supplies the handlines in operation on the roof of this house fire in subzero weather. Winter fires present dangers to firefighters at a scene since the freezing water makes everything slick as . . . ice. Gloves, fittings, and boots become frozen. Southern firefighters have never experienced situations like fire hydrants that don't function because they are frozen. Some northern firefighters prefer winter fires to summer fires since they can prepare for the cold with layers, while the summer heat takes a great toll on them because of the heavy gear they wear.

paramedics. There are pumper designs that also incorporate patient-transport capabilities. As budgets shrink and medical responses increase, fire departments are looking for any means possible to combine duties and continue providing the highest quality of service to the public. In many cases, this is achieved by designing apparatus differently than in years past by equipping pumpers with the supplies necessary to help victims and patients.

Fighting fires is the heart of engine work. Firefighters will use attack lines (or hoses) of varying sizes to handle different fire loads. A small one-room fire will be fought with a 1 1/2- or 1 3/4-inch line while a heavier fire will necessitate a 2 1/2-inch line right from the start. Several attack lines on each pumper are preconnected to the fire pump and are ready to use as soon as they are removed from the engine. These are referred to as pre-connects or cross-lays. The balance of the attack line on the rig is supplemental and used to lengthen the pre-connects, or as additional attack lines.

The number one priority at a fire scene is to put water between the fire and the occupants, allowing for escape and rescue. Once the engine company is in place, it is necessary to cool the highest and hottest point of the fire to prevent inversion, or flashover. Even though each company's work is specific in its tasks, the bottom line at every working fire is that every task supports the nozzle man to get at the seat of the fire. When the structure has more than one floor, the operations inside the building center around keeping control of or "holding" the stairways with a handline to aid in rescues and evacuations.

Training for firefighters stresses the importance of understanding building construction and the behavior of fire. Firefighters need to know what's going on when they begin to attack the fire, and

There were no injuries at this four-alarm fire in Evanston, Illinois, which gutted an entire apartment building. Engine 22's Pierce unit was the first on the scene. The wind carried embers across the street, which ignited several small roof fires.

what is going to happen. Fighting fires is combat. Like any other battle, to win the war you must think like the enemy. The acronym "BAG" sums it up: while studying the fire, determine where it's been, where it's at, and where it's going.

When the first engine company arrives on the scene, the officer, who is in charge of the engine company, begins a size-up to determine what is happening. In order to size up the situation, he or she hopes to have a quick initial view of three sides of the structure, which includes the side of the building as they approach, the front of the building, and the far side as they pull slightly past leaving room for the aerial truck, which stops right in front of the building. At this point, only the rear of the structure has not had a cursory inspection which will occur after preliminary jobs have begun.

Assuming there is a fire, the next step is to determine what is needed to attack this fire. The firefighters need to estimate how much hose is needed to reach the fire, what diameter attack line will be used, and which nozzle. A rule of thumb for the length of hose needed at the front door is to figure 50 feet per floor plus the depth of the building. Determining

One of San Francisco's American LaFrance pumpers connected to the plug after a reverse lay.

After the interior attack was abandoned, the Deerfield, Illinois, Fire Department put the deck gun to work from this Pierce pumper, which was first on the scene.

A firefighter uses the deck gun from an American LaFrance pumper. When the fire becomes a defensive battle and all companies are removed from the building, master streams go to work. The deck gun, which is often prepiped directly to the pump, is a way to deliver a high volume of water from a safe distance.

the diameter of attack line needed is often based on experience. Since a fire can double in size every minute, it may be necessary to look a little ahead. Otherwise, it's simple: a small fire means a small line and a big fire requires a big line. The next decision regards which nozzle to use. Basically, there are two types: a fog nozzle and a smooth board tip (also called a pipe.) A smooth board has less pressure at the tip, which is easier on the firefighters. This can be advantageous for departments with less manpower. The smooth board also provides deeper penetration and superior reach, as compared to a fog nozzle that is set to release a straight stream with the same pressure.

As the officer is deciding what equipment is needed to attack the fire, it is necessary for the engineer to establish a water supply. Connecting a line between an engine and a hydrant is referred to as taking or making a hydrant. Depending on the type of department and the SOPs, there are two different

While the truck company works to ventilate the roof, the engine stands by to charge the handlines. This Pierce engine has a top-mounted operator's console, which offers the engineer an unobstructed view of the entire scene.

operations that can occur to take the nearest hydrant: a reverse lay or a forward lay.

A reverse lay is most common in big cities with sufficient manpower. The officer and firefighters will jump off the rig in front of the building and go to the rear hose beds. Grabbing an armful of hose called a horseshoe, one or more firefighters will pull a 200-foot section of hose off the rig. This will already have a nozzle attached to it. Once completed, the driver, or chauffeur, will drive the rig down the street to the fire hydrant, which is also known as a plug. As the engine goes down the street, hose that is connected to the horseshoe will unravel from the hose bed and snake down the street.

The horseshoe becomes the attack line that the engine crew will stretch to the front door of the structure. At the same time, the engineer separates the hose in the street from the remaining hose in the bed and makes a connection to one of the rig's discharges. The next step is for a large-diameter section of hose to be connected from the engine to the plug, securing an uninterrupted water supply to the pump.

When the engine crew is ready to enter the structure, they contact the engineer via radio and give instructions to charge the attack line. Although this entire process may seem tedious and cumbersome, this can all be achieved in under two or three minutes. It is also possible for the engineer to charge the attack line with the tank water before making the connection to the plug. If all goes well, the engineer can secure the hydrant before the nozzle crew exhausts the entire tank supply.

The reverse lay puts the engine at the hydrant where it can get a higher volume of water into the pumper with greater pressure. Additionally, the rig is out of the way, leaving the front of the building open for one or more aerial devices.

The chauffeur is positioned at the top-mounted operator's control panel awaiting instructions to charge the attack line being taken in through the front door. The truck company is ventilating the roof and second-floor windows.

During a bitter cold day, this vintage Pirsch pumper works from a plug at the end of the block.

When the engineer opens the valves to flow water through the hose, a clear understanding of the physics at hand is necessary. For instance, the longer the distance that the water must travel, the greater the amount of friction loss that occurs along the way. This has to be offset to ensure the appropriate volume or pressure is available at the nozzle to fight the fire. Factors to be considered include the diameter of the hose and whether or not the hose is traveling up stairs to another floor.

Every length of hose owned by a fire department is numbered. When the hose is placed into the hose bed, a list is made of each piece as it is loaded. The engineer can determine how far the hose stretches down the street at a fire by noting the number on the last length of hose that he pulled off the rig. Then, by referring to the inventory list, which keeps track of each length loaded into the bed, he can tell how many lengths came off prior to the last one.

The engineer remains at the pump panel monitoring both the pressure of each handline and the radio for instructions from the nozzle crew. If the company desires more pressure, they'll call for it over the radio. An engineer is cautious not to send too much pressure because the line will be too hard to handle. It's easier to ask for more pressure than for less. If the pressure is too great, the nozzle man may not be able to let go of the hose to speak into the radio and ask for a reduction.

The forward lay positions the rig or "tool box" in front of or very close to the fire building. Here, the engine stops at the hydrant preceding the fire building. One firefighter exits the rig, pulls a length of large-diameter supply line from the hose bed, and wraps it around the hydrant. The engineer then proceeds to drive the rig to a position in front of the structure, laying hose all the time. When the rig stops, the hydrant man makes the hydrant while the engineer disconnects the supply line at the hose bed and reconnects it to one of the rig's intake ports. The hydrant is opened and the water is sent to the

Suburban volunteer firefighters rest after fighting a house fire, and prepare to pick up the handlines. The three engines visible on scene all feature commercial Ford C-8000 cabs.

pumper, which remains close to the building allowing cross-lays, tools, and other equipment to be utilized by the working companies. After the hydrant man finishes with the hydrant, he will join the rest of the company at the structure. This also places the engineer in a position to assist other firefighters with ladders and additional lines, and to exchange air bottles when they are exhausted. Most often, smaller departments will utilize this SOP when they do not have an abundance of manpower.

Cross-lays or speed-lays are preconnected attack lines that are ready to pull off the rig and go into service without having to make any connections. They are often color-coded to the gauges on the pump panel and can be charged in a matter of seconds for a quick hit on the fire.

In some cases, the engine company will make a forward lay without leaving a hydrant man. In this situation, either the engineer has to run back down the street to make the plug, or the next-in company will stop at the hydrant to complete the task while the engine company makes a quick hit using tank water. Another variation to this scenario would be for the first-due engine to bypass the hydrant completely without laying a supply line. They would work off their tank and the next engine company on the scene would back down to the first engine and then make a reverse lay to the hydrant. The engineer of the first engine would connect the supply line to his rig while the second engine makes the plug and stays there.

When one engine pumps water into another engine, this is called in-line pumping. This can boost the pressure from the hydrant to the attack pumper. In-line pumping is also used to draw water from hydrants that are supplied by different water mains and may be farther away, in an effort to increase the capacity of the attack engine.

After the fire is out, every hose must be rolled up and repacked for the next fire.

One facet of the engine, which used to be very popular, is the booster line. Also called a red line, the booster is a rigid rubber hose that winds around a large reel. It is easy to pull and use, and very simple to rewind without much effort. Allowing for a maximum of perhaps 90 gallons per minute, this line is ideal for trash fires and other small fires. Despite the easy-to-use features, many departments have eliminated the booster lines from their rigs. This is due in large part to firefighters who were using the red lines in the wrong situations. Since they are so easy to operate, they were regularly used for fires that should have had a larger-diameter attack line with a 300-gallon-per-minute capacity. Firefighters were getting injured because they did not use the appropriate tool for the task.

Improvements in engine design have increased safety for the firefighting crews while, at the same time making their jobs easier through advancements in engineering, equipment placement, and layout.

CHAPTER 2
AERIALS

After the chief officer determined that an offensive, interior attack was no longer an option, the tower ladder was set up to provide a master stream of 2,000 gallons per minute to douse the fire from a safe distance. Since the tower had its own pump, the crew took a hydrant and went to work high above the scene. With the tower extended only a fraction of its potential, the stream from 30 feet in the air could easily hit the seat of the fire.

Firefighters from Columbus, Wisconsin, operate two handlines and a master stream from their new Pierce tower ladder.

The firefighters in the platform are taking a real beating from the cold and smoke as they work at this extra-alarm fire.

Aerials, commonly referred to as trucks, have a permanently mounted aerial device to provide a means for firefighters to reach the upper floors, or roof, of a building. This device can be a ladder, a ladder with a platform at the end, or an articulating device with a platform. Straight ladders generally extend from 75 to 135 feet and are mounted to a turntable. Placement of the turntable can be in the middle of the vehicle directly behind the cab or, most commonly, at the rear of the truck. When a platform is built at the end of a ladder, the unit is referred to as a tower ladder, ladder tower, or platform aerial and can stretch out 75 to 105 feet from the chassis. Articulating booms are called snorkels, with lengths ranging from 50 to 95 feet. Snorkels have no ladder for walking from the base of the truck to the platform.

Aerials are designed with different performance capabilities. The ladders are made with different strengths to be able to accommodate varying numbers of people at one time. Keeping in mind the angle from the ground and length of extension, the structural weight ratings will vary. The strongest aerials can accommodate a tip load in excess of 500 pounds with the ladder fully extended while parallel to the ground. This is considered the position that places the greatest amount of stress on the ladder. More often than not, reach to the sides is considered more valuable than straight up in the air since the majority of rescue work is performed at lower angles rather than at steeper angles.

Companies currently building trucks are Pierce, Seagrave, LTI, E-One, KME, Snorkel, Aerial Innovations, Smeal, American LaFrance, and Sutphen. Many names can still be found on trucks throughout the country but are no longer in production. Pirsch, Maxim, Grumman, FMC, Ward LaFrance, and Grove are some of the more widely visible nameplates. Similar to the manufacture of engines, trucks can be built by a single source from the bottom up, or they can consist of a chassis, body, and aerial device from different suppliers. Foreign companies also manufacture aerial trucks overseas, but these units rarely are built to the stringent specifications required by the NFPA.

Fire trucks need to conform to state and federal guidelines covering the vehicle's weight, placement of emergency lighting, emissions, and fuel consumption, in addition to the requirements that are placed by the NFPA, which often target personnel safety. Fire trucks are not exempt from requirements placed on other trucks. Sometimes state laws and national

Firefighters control the master stream from a midship Seagrave aerial as fire breaks through the roof of a commercial building. The large-diameter hose running up the sections of ladder supplies the deck gun working at the tip. Since this is a straight truck with no pump, an engine supplies the water.

A Pierce TDA works at an apartment building fire.

guidelines will conflict. One example covers emergency lighting. The NFPA requires the placement of amber revolving lights on the rear of units, at the top of the body. The state of Maryland does not allow amber lights on fire trucks. In order to comply with the NFPA, the truck manufacturers deliver the units with the amber lights to protect themselves from litigation, but upon receipt of the vehicles in Maryland, the dealer or department removes the amber domes and replaces them with red domes so the vehicles conform to the state law.

Some states demand special certifications and rigid testing for all aerials. Occasionally, an aerial device fails, resulting in an injury or death to the firefighters or civilians on the ladder. This results in a thorough review of procedures and policies in fire departments around the country to ensure that the tragedy is not repeated elsewhere. Nationally, aerials must be tested and certified on a regular basis to ensure the structural integrity of the unit, guaranteeing the safety of those who will use it.

Ladders

Aerial ladders can be made of aluminum or steel. The majority of builders use steel, although aluminum is very popular. If the turntable where the ladder originates is right behind the cab, the unit is

Five of Chicago's tower ladders were working at this 5-11 alarm fire. Here, TL10 prepares to put its HME/LTI apparatus to work with a master stream.

referred to as a midmount, or midship aerial. The ladder on a midship hangs past the rear of the vehicle. Popular in the 1970s, midships represented state-of-the-art aerial design. It was a trend that was largely industry-driven. In other words, that's what was available. Few companies today build a midship aerial, although several are building midship towers. One of the benefits of a midship design is that it provides a lower overall traveling height of the vehicle. Since the ladder is not higher than the truck's cab, the unit can fit into older fire stations with low 10- or 11-foot doors.

A rear mount was the next generation of aerials to be introduced. These have the turntable at the back of the chassis, and rest the ladder over the cab of the truck. The introduction of rear-mounted aerials brought greater maneuverability without the rear overhang of the ladder. If a driver was not careful leaving a fire house with a midship aerial, it was possible to hit the station doorway with the ladder as they were turning.

A third design is called a tractor-drawn aerial (TDA), which is a two-piece vehicle consisting of a tractor and separate trailer. The ladder is mounted at the front of the trailer, and at the back is a position for a tillerman who steers the rear wheels. Tillers have been around since the 1950s and are still popular. Since the truck is so long, maneuverability at the rear is essential. Actually, a TDA is the truck of choice for many older cities, because narrow streets that have an abundance of parked cars and other obstacles prevent longer "straight-frame" trucks from getting around easily.

Every truck has some type of stabilizer to keep the vehicle from tipping over when the ladder works off one side of the vehicle. Builders use two, four, or even five stabilizers. Whether they move out to the side of the truck and down like big legs, emerge from

The versatility of an articulating Aero Chief Snorkel is displayed at this winter fire. The bucket permits the firefighters to sweep back and forth hitting hot spots.

35

underneath and stay low, or simply move straight down, each design is an important part of the structural integrity and safety of the truck. The stabilizers on a ladder truck will often have a shorter outward spread than other types of aerials since they have a lower-weight capacity at the tip.

Aerial ladders consist of three to five sections that will nest within the base section. As the ladder extends, each section begins to telescope away from the turntable until the desired distance is reached. The end section is called the fly section and may be equipped to flow water when an elevated master stream is required. Controls for the ladder are located at the turntable and may also be available at the tip of the fly section or, in some cases, at the operator's panel for units with a pump. An intercom system allows for garbled conversation between the turntable and the tip of the ladder. Many fire departments store the tools needed most often along the sides of the ladder. These include an ax, pike pole, and Stokes basket for removing an injured victim.

In economic terms, a ladder truck is less expensive and lighter in overall weight than a platform aerial.

Platforms

Another aerial design adds a platform that can hold three or four firefighters at the end of the ladder. Instead of walking up the ladder, the firefighters can all ascend to the roof by entering the platform from the ground and riding up on the platform. Once the aerial is up in the air, firefighters can use the ladder as a means to go back and forth between the ground and the platform. Many departments have been replacing aerial ladders with tower ladders because it is easier to rescue victims and faster when sending several firefighters to the roof of a building. When occupants need to be removed from the upper floors of a fire building, firefighters would rather place them into a platform for the trip to the ground as opposed to having to walk each person down a ladder. Any civilian who walks down a ladder must be accompanied by a firefighter. When the civilians are

cold, wet, scared, or suffering from exposure to smoke, walking down a ladder backward is an additional unsettling experience. Platforms can move from window to window rescuing victims. Only under extreme cases would an aerial ladder be moved between windows unless everyone was off the ladder. Platform aerials have greater tip load capacities, up to 2,000 pounds, and require heavier subframes.

During a defensive attack at a large fire, the aerial will be extended above the fire with a large water stream directed at the seat of the fire. An aerial ladder requires one firefighter to either rest on a special step at the tip of the ladder to direct the stream, or use a rope trailing to the ground, which allows the firefighter to direct the water flow. A platform allows the same firefighter to remain standing and even get relieved by other firefighters without having to make major adjustments or shut down the water, allowing for more accurate direction of the master stream with instantaneous results. Tower ladders can be midship mounted or rear mounted.

Articulating Devices

A snorkel refers to an articulating aerial device with a bucket at the end. The solid boom does not provide a ladder, so the only way to get from the ground to the upper floors and roof is to travel in the bucket. Preferred by some over a tower ladder, the snorkel provides versatility that is not available with a telescoping aerial. The snorkel allows over and under access that cannot be achieved by taking a straight path. Like the other aerials, a snorkel has a prepiped waterway along the boom that allows for an elevated master water stream.

In an effort to combine the best traits of a snorkel with those of a tower ladder, several companies have developed new designs. One allows the fly section to articulate down at an angle from the rest

A Snorkel reaches up and over the trees, allowing firefighters to get at the fire burning through the roof of a commercial building.

QUINTS

Generally, a truck refers to a unit that has an aerial device and portable ground ladders. Some trucks are equipped with fire pumps and water tanks similar to an engine. When this is the case, the unit is referred to as a quint. A quint has five distinct qualities that merit this classification. First of all, the unit has a permanently mounted aerial device. Next, the unit carries a minimum of 115 feet of portable ground ladders in addition to a minimum of 500 gallons of water. The fourth requirement is a pump with at least a 750-gallon-per-minute capacity, and finally, the unit must have the capacity to carry 1,500 cubic feet of fire hose. Many quints today fall short of the full classification because the water tanks are reduced to between 250 and 300 gallons of water. The additional weight for the added water makes the bigger trucks too heavy for some street restrictions and causes excessive wear on the vehicle.

Quints have become both popular and controversial. The popularity stems from the added capabilities available on the fireground that these units provide. Some departments use the quint as a first-due unit since it has water to make an initial attack on the fire, while others have gone to the total quint concept. Simply put, every unit in the fleet is a quint. They can respond and work as an engine or a truck depending on the situation upon arrival. The first unit arriving works as an engine while the second unit handles truck responsibilities. Companies are cross-trained to handle either type of assignment. In small departments, manpower may prohibit the ability to get two rigs out the door for an initial response. In this case, the quint can act as the initial rig on reported structure fires, which provides

Above
Since the first unit on the scene was this Pierce quint, the Arlington Heights, Illinois, Fire Department was able to utilize the pre-connects to make a quick hit on a room and contents fire before it got out of control.

Facing page, top
A Sutphen pumper supplies several preconnected handlines fighting this grocery store fire, in addition to a large-diameter supply line, which runs to the E-One quint. The firefighter working the nozzle at the tip of the prepiped waterway has a special step to support him while he works.

Facing page, bottom
Firefighters repack hose on a quint after a fire in St. Louis. Using the quint concept, the first-arriving unit performs the functions of an engine company while the next unit works as a truck.

the first-arriving company with the capability to begin rescues from the upper floors or to take a hydrant and begin advancing an attack line until the next unit arrives.

Quint controversy comes in several forms. One of the most stringent adversaries is tradition. When the lines between engine and truck companies become blurred, firefighters fight the loss of control and direction that they once had. Complaints arise that cross-training dilutes the abilities of the companies to perform at their optimal potential by changing the tasks that they perform from fire to fire. Unions can also present an obstacle to the use of quints. Often the chauffeur of an engine who serves as the pump operator carries a different job classification than other firefighters. Unions feel that an engineer is required for the operation of the quint, where management often feels that the unit is more of a truck and fights the use of an engineer.

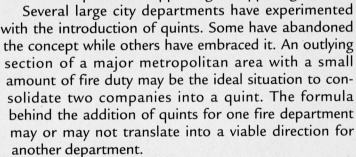

Some fire departments utilize quints as a means to consolidate two companies (an engine and a truck) into one. This single company requires fewer personnel than the two separate companies, which lowers the expense for the department but threatens job security for some firefighters. Although each of these arguments has merit, each has counterarguments with equal merit supporting the opposing views.

Several large city departments have experimented with the introduction of quints. Some have abandoned the concept while others have embraced it. An outlying section of a major metropolitan area with a small amount of fire duty may be the ideal situation to consolidate two companies into a quint. The formula behind the addition of quints for one fire department may or may not translate into a viable direction for another department.

The City of St. Louis Fire Department uses the full quint concept and serves as a model for other cities nationwide. Richmond, Virginia, has also adopted quints. The City of Baltimore is one department that experimented with quints and has abandoned the program.

Using chain saws, a truck crew works off ladders to expose the fire, which is hidden underneath the roof.

the distance between a piece of aerial apparatus and the burning building. Most often, the greatest obstacle is not vertical height, but horizontal reach. Trucks need sufficient space for outriggers and stabilizers, in addition to a secure surface underneath, ensuring the safety of the firefighters and the rig. New housing developments and office parks frequently place the buildings a great distance from the parking lot to enhance the external appeal. For the fire department, this means longer distances to carry equipment and park their apparatus in the event of an emergency.

Duties

Truck companies have different duties than those of an engine company. At a structure fire, the engine company deals with extinguishing the flames with water. The truck company's responsibilities include search and rescue, ventilation, and forcible entry. Every fire department's primary role is the protection of lives and property. As the engine company secures a water source and advances handlines, the truck company may first need to forcibly gain access to the building with sledge hammers, axes, or pry bars. Next is the need to conduct a primary search for victims if entry is possible. A painstaking process of crawling through a smoky building with zero visibility is often the manner of a primary or immediate search and rescue of the occupants.

As the initial search for victims is being conducted, other truck work needs to be handled concurrently. A building needs to be ventilated, permitting the smoke and hot gases from the fire to escape, which lets the engine company advance on the fire. Windows are broken and holes are cut in the roof. When the smoke is allowed to escape from the confines of the building through selected paths, the engine crews have increased visibility and reduced heat, allowing them to better tolerate the interior conditions and work. Ventilation also helps the crews performing the search operations for the same reasons. These operations are optimized when a sufficient number

of the ladder after it has been extended. This allows firefighters to lower the platform behind a parapet wall or other obstacle that hampers placement of the platform for safe egress. Another design incorporates two separate joints that allow the boom to articulate with precision at heights up to 160 feet. The more capabilities an aerial device offers, the higher the expense will be to purchase that vehicle.

People sometimes wonder why smaller departments are buying apparatus with longer aerial devices even though they have no building in their district higher than two or three stories. The reason for this is simple, though not always obvious. Parked cars, landscaping, and small driveways all increase of personnel are on the scene so these tasks can be performed simultaneously.

To emphasize how important ventilation is to the entire operation, consider this bit of information. In the 1970s, one pound of combustible materials emitted 8,000 BTUs of heat production. Today, due in large part to the extra levels of hydrocarbons in all products, that same one pound of combustibles produces 18,000 to 22,000 BTUs of heat—double or triple the amount of heat found twenty years ago. Unattacked, a fire doubles every minute. Smoke explodes when it is in an oxygen-deprived area. As the heat levels increase and the fire consumes the oxygen in the building, the potential for an explosion, flashover, or backdraft increases significantly. Ventilation gives the hot gases an escape route. It's all summed up with the acronym "VES": vent, enter, and search for the occupants and the fire. When found, rescue the occupants, contain, confine, and extinguish the fire.

Another element adding to the urgency and importance of adequate ventilation is the fact that a firefighter's protective clothing is currently rated up to temperatures of 1,500 degrees. Fires today can produce temperatures from 1,700 to 2,000 degrees.

Although engines carry a few ground ladders, trucks are equipped with more ladders of varying sizes. The truck company will use either portable ground ladders or the aerial device of their apparatus to gain access to the roof for ventilation. The truck crew will also access the upper floors for the rescue of occupants or the escape of firefighters. The worst scenario for firefighters arriving at a building with heavy fire and smoke is to find residents at windows on every floor shouting for help. The first companies have to make fast decisions. Often, the first order of business will be to get all of the available ground ladders from the truck, along with those from the engines on the scene, and throw them up to the windows quickly. Even though a firefighter will not be available to climb the ladders right away, many victims will work on their own to get out once a ladder

has been placed at their window. Given the choice between climbing down the ladder without a firefighter or staying in the room with the fast-approaching fire, most people will make the obvious choice.

Like any fire crew, truck companies will have both departmental and individual protocols or SOPs. Large departments with a sufficient manning of six firefighters will generally have three teams of two each with specific tasks upon arrival. These tasks will not have to be discussed unless a deviation is required by the truck officer or incident commander. Two to the roof, two to the front, and two to the rear is a pretty routine assignment. When only four personnel make up the truck company, a single-family dwelling will require two in the front, and the other two to inspect the exterior and head to the rear before going to the roof. A multifamily building will mean that the entire truck crew of four will begin search and rescue operations. They will move ahead of the engine company to force entry. The search

A Snorkel unit prepares to go to work at a four-alarm fire in an apartment complex.

Firefighters maneuver the master stream from the turntable of this Pierce aerial to attack the fire, which consumed an entire block of stores.

companies will mark the doors of each unit or use some sort of item to keep the door from locking so that other companies know that the rooms have been searched.

Placement of the apparatus (also known as spotting) by the chauffeur upon arrival is extremely important. Should the fixed aerial device need to go into service, the vehicle must be placed in a position where it is ready. Quite often, building setbacks (the distance between the structure and the pavement) and size render even the largest aerial devices only remotely effective. A fire above the eighth floor of a high-rise is generally unreachable from the ground.

Standard protocols state that the truck takes the address of the building, meaning the front door. The driver places the turntable of the aerial device in a position that allows access to work the building in the event of rescues. The aerial must be placed in the best position to "wash" the building, plucking residents from their windows or balconies as it "scrubs" individual floors. The first priority is to rescue the people on higher floors because of the risk that they might try to jump. Ground ladders will handle the lower floors.

It might not seem obvious, but even the manner in which a ladder is raised to a window is important.

Assisting the engine crew inside the building, the truck company works off the ladder to ventilate the roof and attic area of this mansion.

Firefighters will bring the ladder alongside a window, and then over to the victim instead of directly to the victim. This is an attempt to prevent premature jumping or grabbing for the ladder by the victim before it is in place. This is true with both ground ladders and the main fixed aerial device. In a panic, people do irrational things.

If an aerial ladder will be used to its fullest extent, the most stable position is straight off the back, and in-line with the frame rails of the chassis. At a high-rise fire, a truck's best position is to take the corner of the building, for several reasons. First of all, this gives the truck crew access to two sides of the building with their ladders for rescues. Additionally, the corner of the structure is the strongest part of the building and will protect the apparatus in the event the building collapses.

When the truck company performs their search from the building's interior, standard procedures call for the following search order: first, the fire floor, followed by the floor immediately above the fire floor, and then the top floor. The reason for skipping any floors in between is that convected air brings poisonous gases to the highest floor, placing these occupants in imminent danger. These toxic and harmful vapors require that all firefighters use SCBAs for their own protection.

Departments that run with more than one truck company will have SOPs for the first-in truck company that differ from the second-due truck. Generally, the second truck will arrive and park farther from the scene unless the incident commander requests their apparatus right away. Firefighters will report to the fire building with truck tools. These consist of pike poles, axes, and saws. After assisting the first truck with ventilation of the roof, they will assist with a secondary search for victims, check for extension of the fire, and begin salvage and overhaul work.

Working off the rear of this American LaFrance aerial, a ladder pipe goes to work as the fire takes control of the top floor. Since this is not a prepiped rig, a section of large-diameter hose needed to be run up the ladder to a pipe at the tip of the fly section.

A 1961 open-cab Seagrave 85-foot midship ladder works at a five-alarm fire using an elevated master stream.

Two elevated master streams from aerial ladders are already at work as this tower ladder backs into position to add another master stream.

Secondary searches are more thorough than the primary searches, which are often conducted under less than ideal conditions. During the secondary search, smoke and heat will factor much less into the operation, allowing for improved visibility to conduct the search. The primary search may have been conducted solely by feel due to zero visibility.

Overhaul is the process of checking for fire extension with pike poles and axes by going over the area where the engine companies extinguished the fire. Since fire conceals itself inside walls and ceilings, the truck company will "pull" ceilings and walls in an effort to chase the fire or head it off before it travels farther. They will also poke through any debris to check for "hot spots" or areas of hidden fire. Only when they feel that all the fire's extension throughout the building has been halted is the fire declared to be out. One can often spot the truckies leaving a

Chicago TL-10 reaches over the elevated rail tracks to pour water on a 5-11 alarm fire on the city's north side.

After ventilating the roof, allowing the fire and smoke to escape from the house, firefighters prepare to put a handline to use.

building. They're the ones with the air masks or faces covered with drywall dust and debris from pulling ceilings while looking up.

Salvage—protecting building contents from water and smoke damage—is also truck work. During the fire, if the department's SOPs specify salvage work, large canvas tarps will be used to protect furniture and other contents from water damage on the floors below the fire. This may also be done after the fire has been extinguished and can involve removing some contents from the structure for the tenants or owners. If the building is unsafe for civilians, the truck company will assist the occupants to whatever degree they can in order to reclaim valuables.

If an interior attack of the fire is ineffective or not possible due to a high volume of fire on arrival, then the truck company's apparatus may be put into service as an aerial master stream. In this event, the position of the vehicle is again important. First of all, it needs to be positioned where the master stream will be able to do some good. Additionally, should the building become unstable and collapse, the apparatus must be placed outside of the collapse zone.

For the average person, the most dramatic aspects of firefighting might rest with the engine crews manning the handlines to extinguish the fire. Much of the work done by the truck company either goes unseen from the outside or appears destructive during ventilation. In reality, the work of each company is vital to the successful outcome of the battle. Truck work is exciting, hard, and rewarding. There can be no comparison to the emotions experienced by making a successful rescue from a fire scene.

47

CHAPTER 3
TANKERS

W*orkers scrambled as fire broke out at a commercial coffee dis-tribution center in an area without hydrants. A call went out for a tanker shuttle, which sustained this firefight by using 15 units with a combined capacity of over 30,000 gallons of water. Several portable tanks were tied together allowing two pumpers to draft simultaneously, supplying water for elevated master streams along with several deck guns. The aroma of coffee filled the air as the fire burned for 6 hours.*

Large fires require huge amounts of water to keep multiple master streams operating. Two tankers simultaneously dump their water into side-by-side portable tanks.

The primary function of a tanker is to carry large amounts of water to areas that do not have a permanent or steady water supply. Often similar to the tank trucks seen carrying milk, gasoline, or other bulk liquids, fire tankers are responsible for bringing the equivalent of several engines' worth of water to a fire scene. Rural areas, remote locations, or undeveloped sections of a community frequently do not have a stable water supply available to the fire department.

Developed areas have an underground system of water mains connected every half block to a plug. In this environment, the engines simply connect to the hydrant and draw water, which is pumped through the engine into the hoses. Until the engine is securely fastened to the hydrant, the tank water is used to sustain a brief attack. Even the largest pumpers, though, with 1,000 gallons of tank water, cannot last very long considering a handline can use up to 350 gallons per minute. If a steady water supply is not established, the line firefighters are in danger of injury, and the potential exists for sustained damage to the property they are trying to protect.

Tankers respond to districts that do not have hydrants, and carry between 1,000 and 6,000 gallons of water with the ability to unload or dump their supply very rapidly. Large discharge tubes appropriately called "dumps" are incorporated into the tanks to release the water quickly. When the tank is empty, the rig will travel to a location with a water supply to refill before returning to the scene. Ideally, when one tanker leaves, another pulls up to the engine and stands ready to dump its load. Next in line, another unit waits its turn. This is referred to as a tanker

After backing into position, a firefighter opens the rear dump valve of a 3,200-gallon elliptical tanker to fill the portable tank.

This tractor-trailer tanker carries 6,000 gallons of water and is called to the scene of an extra-alarm commercial building fire in an area that has no fire hydrants.

shuttle. Each unit dumps its load, then leaves to fill up and return.

The biggest tankers are tractor-trailer combinations. Using conventional over-the-road tractors without sleepers, shiny, elliptical, stainless-steel tankers can hold up to 6,000 gallons of water. Smaller units can have several different designs, although the elliptical style is common. Capacities of 3,500 to 4,000 gallons will require a tandem rear axle and generally feature a commercial truck chassis.

Tankers with 1,000- to 3,000-gallon capacities often look like very big engines and are referred to as pumper-tankers. The tanks are located within the vehicle's body and are surrounded by compartments for tools and accessories just like an engine. These units can be differentiated from regular pumpers by the tandem rear axles and significantly higher bodies. They are set up as engines but carry the larger water loads to perform the dual function of both units. One side of the unit generally holds a portable tank. When a pumper-tanker pulls up to a working fire, the bigger water tank provides a larger window of time for the pump operator to secure a continuous water supply while the firefighters operate handlines.

Like engines, pumper-tankers can have fully enclosed cabs with seating for up to 10 firefighters.

51

Here is an example of a tanker with the operator's controls mounted at the front of the unit.

The pump controls can be on the unit's side or on top, providing a full view of the scene for the engineer. Custom or commercial cabs and chassis are used along with a variety of pump capacities. Although the pump controls are generally midship, some units have the pump controls located on an extended front bumper. Air packs, hand tools, fans, large-diameter hose, preconnected handlines, and nozzles fill the compartments just like a conventional engine.

Units that are set up strictly as tankers have smaller pumps than those found in engines. There is no need to spend the additional money for a full-size pump when the rig will not be used as a pumping source. If designed properly, gravity handles most of the duties of dumping the tank, and any supplemental pumping can be handled at 350 as opposed to

An elliptical tanker from Wauconda, Illinois, with a Ford Louisville chassis stands ready at a house fire.

53

Firefighters break down one of the portable tanks used at a fire in a nonhydranted area.

1,500 gallons per minute. These smaller pumps are power take-off, or PTO, pumps, and work off a power take-off opening in the truck's transmission. In the event that a portable tank is not used and the water in a tanker is sufficient for the required purpose, then another procedure may be used, called nursing the tanker. Here, a pumper hooks up directly to the tanker for the water supply, similar to hooking up to a hydrant. Everything else runs normally.

Most tankers carry a portable, collapsible tank, which looks much like an aboveground swimming pool. The collapsible tank is stored on the side of the

An FMC pumper with a custom chassis is one of two engines drafting out of a portable tank supplying attack lines to the aerials that are visible in the background. Three portable tanks are tied together to provide an uninterrupted water supply.

tanker. These tanks can hold from 1,000 to 3,000 gallons of water. The first tanker on scene will have its crew quickly assemble a tank on the street while the engine's pump operator prepares to draft water to supply the handlines. The portable tank is generally designed to hold more water than is carried in the tanker. Many fire departments will set up multiple portable tanks and link them together, guaranteeing a greater available supply. A tanker will dump its water into the portable tank and then move to the area that has been designated for refilling. Depending on the area, the filling station can be several miles away. Travel time to and from the filling area will be a factor in determining how many tankers are required at the scene. Tankers are designed with dump tubes on the rear of the tank and can be supplemented with dump tubes on the rig's sides. These side dumps ensure quick unloading and save time by positioning the rig alongside the portable tanks. If the tanker has to back up to the tank, extra time is required. The ability to unload a tanker's water in minutes is essential for a smooth tanker shuttle.

Here's how it works. When an alarm is sounded in an area without a water supply, one or more tankers will respond with the engine company. If a fire is discovered, additional tankers will be called to the scene. The command unit will establish a water supply officer to ensure adequate quantities of water are available to support the handlines and master streams at work. Another officer will be assigned the task of locating and establishing a place for refilling the tankers.

Tankers travel in the emergency mode with lights and sirens to and from the refilling location. An engine is assigned at the refilling spot to pump water into the tankers. Perhaps they will be working off a hydrant system from a neighboring incorporated area or municipality. Other possibilities are lakes, rivers, or ponds where the engine will draft water. Unlike using a hydrant that has water pressure, a body of water requires the engine to pull or draft the water through a large-diameter, rigid rubber hose.

When fire hydrants are not available, it becomes necessary to find alternate sources of water to supply the attack units and aerials. Here, a pumper drafts water from a pond.

Volunteer firefighters in suburban Detroit rest after fighting a barn fire.

The hose is placed into the water source with a large screen over the open end. This is to ensure that nothing but water and very small particles are sucked into and through the engine's pump, because large foreign items would cause damage to the fire pump, disabling the unit.

It is not uncommon in distant rural areas to augment the fire department's tankers with privately owned water tankers. If neighboring fire departments are located too far away to respond in an acceptable amount of time, these private tankers will be called into action at large fires. Not unlike the civilian patrols that assist government agencies with the search for downed aircraft, these civilians aid the fire department in times of need. In order to perform this function, the private water tankers have to meet various criteria, which include warning lights and the ability to dump the entire load quickly. The owners will not be involved in any firefighting capacities, just in the duties of maintaining the water supply.

Unlike an engine or truck company with a crew of three to six people, a tanker will generally respond with two firefighters. One is, of course, the driver, and the other assists with hookups for dumping and refilling. In addition, since tankers are large vehicles, the second person assists the driver while they maneuver through the tight spots in which they frequently find themselves. Manpower for fighting the fire comes from engine, truck, and squad companies.

Speed is very important in tanker operations. The quicker the tanker crew can hook up, the quicker they can dump their water, making sure that the water supply for fighting the fire is uninterrupted. Tanker operations are represented by long lines of tankers waiting their turn at the portable tanks. At large fires, as many as 15 tankers can be seen in line.

The backbone of a tanker shuttle is the line of tankers waiting to dump their water. Although the work may seem boring, it is an essential aspect of rural firefighting.

Two tankers are awaiting instructions at the dump site where two portable tanks are tied together. One pumper is drafting water and sending it down the block to the attack pumper.

Many tanker crews participate in competitions to win the title of fastest hookups and dumps. (These competitions are not at the scene of a fire.) Numerous trophies line the shelves of the departments that take these competitions seriously. The ability to "make-and-break" quickly is imperative to efficient tanker ops. "Make-and-break" refers to making the connection to the water supply for filling the tanker, and then breaking that same connection to return to the scene. Some rural areas have installed permanent fill stations with overhead pipes that can fill at a rate of 5,000 gallons per minute. These fill stations resemble the setups used for the old steam locomotives.

Tanker operations are a highly specialized facet of firefighting. Those who are not familiar with these procedures and have never had to test them may take for granted the simplicity of a smooth tanker shuttle. The fact of the matter is that behind an efficient tanker operation is a carefully planned event resulting from rigid training and precise preparations. Ensuring an uninterrupted water supply is vital to any fire fight, guaranteeing the safety of personnel to protect lives and property. A tanker shuttle is not as exciting as advancing a line to knock down the fire, but is every bit as important to the final outcome.

CHAPTER 4
RESCUE SQUADS

I t was the middle of a bitter cold winter night when fire broke out in a barn, which had been converted into a private antique auto museum. Six fire departments responded immediately, fighting the elements in an attempt to save as many cars as possible. Firefighters had trouble crossing an open field adjacent to the barn because of the deep snow until a rescue squad was set up to light the area, allowing them to see where they were going. Due to the cold temperatures, ice formed on every surface including the firefighters' helmets, coats, and boots, making the entire scene treacherous.

Utilizing two powerful light towers, this rescue squad is positioned to illuminate a scene that would otherwise be dangerous for the firefighters.

Not all fire trucks carry water, hoses, and ladders. As a matter of fact, some units may only resemble other fire trucks by the colors, emergency lights, and the department name on the side. These units are referred to as squads, rescues, rescue squads, heavy-duty rescues, special operations units, or one of several other descriptions. More so than pumpers or aerials, these specialized units have different outward appearances. For simplicity, all such units will be referred to as rescue squads in this chapter, and the firefighters who run with them as the squad company. The unifying factor with each of these vehicles is that they are big tool boxes. Hand tools, special power tools, and life-saving equipment fill the compartments on these trucks.

Basically, there are two different styles of rescue squads. One type is referred to as a walk-in, while the other is a nonwalk-in. A walk-in has storage compartments on the outside of the truck's body plus an interior space with additional storage and room for the crew. The squad company may travel to the scene in the cab or the body section. Nonwalk-in bodies have deeper compartments, which may span the entire width of the truck. In these units, all access to the equipment and supplies is from the exterior and all crew seating is in the cab. In addition to equipment

Prospect Heights, Illinois, runs this Pierce, dubbed "Squadzilla" because of its size, as a heavy rescue, light, air, and pumper/squad unit. In front of the fire building, it supplies several pre-connects in addition to lighting the scene with a telescoping light tower.

stored in compartments on the sides of the vehicle, some rescue squads have under-body compartments and extra compartments on the roof. Rescue squads may be large, elaborate, and custom built, or they can be converted bread trucks, used beverage trucks, or smaller trucks associated with plumbers and other tradesmen.

Chicago operates three squad companies, which have utilized trucks with snorkel aerial devices for many years. These Snorkel Squads respond to working fires, vehicle accidents, and other nonfire emergencies throughout the city limits. Currently, one of these squads runs with a walk-in rescue without a snorkel. Boston operates two walk-in style rescue companies available to respond to emergencies citywide. Providence, Rhode Island, runs a special operations unit. This company handles ordinary and unique incidents requiring extra manpower or specialized tools, equipment, and training.

One department that uses a drastically different type of apparatus for its rescue squad is the Los Angeles City Fire Department. Here, Heavy Rescue 56 operates with a heavy-duty wrecker responding to traffic accidents throughout the city. The unit has a 40-ton hydraulic boom, which can rotate and extend to lift vehicles that have trapped their occupants.

Differing by department, rescue squads respond to many types of calls. In New York City, the FDNY utilizes five rescue companies with walk-in bodies, one in each borough of the city. The rescues respond to all 10-75 runs (confirmed fires), all occurrences where people are trapped, water rescues, hazardous materials incidents, and a multitude of other assignments. Initially, these units were designed solely to assist and rescue other firefighters; now, however, their duties have greatly expanded. Each rescue has a specialty and is backed up by supplemental apparatus to carry additional equipment and supplies. In addition to the five rescues, the FDNY also operates seven squad companies. The squads have traditional pumpers as their assigned apparatus, responding to fires providing supplemental manpower.

FDNY Rescue 5 picks up after responding to a call in Manhattan. All five rescue units run with identical HME/Saulsbury units.

In smaller departments, the use of rescue squads varies greatly. Some departments have vehicles that are not manned full time, but will be special-called to the scene of an incident requiring the equipment they carry. These rescue squads can be manned by off-duty personnel, or an engine/truck company will be taken out of service so their personnel can become the squad company. Other departments have full-time squad companies equivalent to the ones used by larger departments. Often, smaller departments will share resources with neighboring departments, and one rescue squad will be manned responding to calls in several different jurisdictions. Referred to as automatic or mutual aid, each department now has a rescue squad available when they need it.

A rescue squad may be designed for seating as few as 5 people to as many as 10. Depending on the configuration of the cab and body, the vehicle can act as a means to transport many firefighters to a scene, providing supplemental personnel. A large crew area is also invaluable at prolonged incidents, or during inclement weather, to offer a space for rehabilitation and rest for the firefighters.

The key to most rescue squads, and often the greatest source of pride for the company members, is the organization of the vehicle. The saying about putting 10 pounds of stuff in a 5-pound bag emulates

Rescue squads carry an assortment of specialized tools to overcome any obstacles that they encounter. Several tools are visible during this rescue including hydraulic spreaders and cutters, two types of saws, and a special tool that pulls the steering column from the dashboard.

what goes on when a department designs a rescue squad. There is always new equipment, a new tool, or additional items that the rescue squad deems necessary to include. It is imperative that everything be laid out carefully. When the rescue squad arrives on the scene, seconds count if someone's life is at stake.

The extent that many departments go to when laying out and mounting the equipment in a rescue squad is truly an art form. Utilizing drawers on rollers, tool boards that slide in side by side, trays that roll out and down on an angle for easier access, unique compartment shapes, sizes, and color-coding produce vehicles that are extraordinary. For both the fire department and the truck manufacturer, experience is the guide for anyone laying out a rescue squad.

A feature built into numerous suburban rescue squads is a command center. Many units will have cabs with a raised roof, allowing people to stand up and walk around without hitting their heads. This area is perfect for a radio console, a desk, and a chair for the incident commander to spread out the necessary charts and diagrams. Cellular phones and computers are commonplace. Command centers can also be in the walk-in body of a rescue squad, making these same features available to the officer in charge of the scene.

It might seem odd to consider that big-city rescue squads are not always the best equipped nor do they receive the most formal training. Large departments have to spread their resources over a vast array of personnel, equipment, and apparatus. They have enormous responsibilities to provide training for all of the firefighters. Because of this, specialized training may have to take a back seat to the routine training and refresher classes that everyone must have in order to perform their duties. Some rescue company members in big departments will seek training on their own. Their tools and equipment are not always the newest. Occasionally, the need to scrounge presents itself in order to supplement the items of standard issue. Some big-city rescue squads have been handling unique and specialized rescues for years with limited resources.

After a fire, personnel report to this Pierce squad to refill their SCBA.

Suburban and county departments may have the resources to keep their rescue squads up to date with the latest technology, in addition to providing their personnel with constant training. These rescue squads may also have fancier trucks that are laid out perfectly.

Tools

The equipment carried by each unit can be as diverse as the outside appearance of the trucks. Some units are more specialized than others and may be designed for specific tasks. Heavy rescue and extrication, lighting, salvage, hazardous materials, and air systems can be combined together or singled out as the sole purpose for these rigs.

Lighting is imperative to assist with night scenes. A vehicle can be outfitted primarily for the task of providing supplemental light, or this can be incorporated into a heavy rescue unit. Generally equipped with quartz lights, many rescue squads will have pole-mounted lights that can be extended and rotated in any direction. In addition to the pole-mounted lights, portable lights with 500- or 1,000-watt capacities and long cord reels will attach to

large generators, allowing firefighters to bring lights into a building or closer to a rescue scene. Older lighting units were incandescent flood types, which were used before the quartz lights become readily available. Other options include specially designed light towers with up to 6,000-watt outputs. These remote-controlled towers can be extended 16 to 42 feet above the truck, and rotated 360 degrees to provide even illumination of an entire scene.

Providing electric power for lights and tools requires generators with capacities ranging from 5 to 20 kilowatts (kW). Often these generators will be used in addition to portable gas-powered units that can be carried closer to the scene when the use of long cords is not possible.

Firefighters utilize SCBA during a fire. Each bottle of air that they use is rated for 30–60 minutes of use, a rating that is affected by the individual's breathing habits. Each bottle needs to be refilled in preparation for the next fire. Since all vehicles carry spare bottles, some departments require the companies to refill their bottles at a fire station. Others will bring mobile air systems to the scene to refill bottles, or they may have units that carry many bottles to replace those used at a scene. The empty bottles will then be refilled elsewhere.

Whether the unit is solely an air unit, or the filling capabilities are incorporated into a rescue squad, the system is the same. The refilling station is called a cascade system, and varies by the capacity of the cylinders. The system consists of as few as one large air cylinder to as many as six cylinders filled with compressed air. The fill station is a system of gauges and air lines to connect the SCBA bottles to the refill cylinders. This operation can be done while the bottle

Filling air bottles is often the bulk of the work performed by many suburban rescue squads. After the fire is out, this becomes the primary duty.

As one car burns, crews from two rescue squads cut open a second car to gain access to the trapped occupant using a maneuver called a "reverse Noah's Arc," which means the rescue squads create a hinged ramp-like access panel out of the car doors and surrounding sheet metal. Since the car is upside down, the operation is called a reverse.

THE COMPANY

What kind of person works on a rescue squad? Most often, squad members request this duty as opposed to being assigned here. Rescue squads handle more runs than engines and trucks, and these firefighters *want* to be kept busy. They may have a higher level of motivation than others because they have chosen to be here. If there is a fire or other incident, they are usually "chomping at the bit," waiting to be called to the scene. They will respond to confirmed fires more frequently than other companies and are more likely to go to work and keep busy at a fire. Since they are busier, they have more experience, enabling them to assist other firefighters. In many cases, squad members are the "go to" guys. They are there to help other firefighters. They are not necessarily any better than other firefighters, just more experienced because they've done the jobs more often. They need to adapt, improvise, and overcome their surroundings so they can handle any situation.

Not all firefighters have the experience, the ability, or the desire to aggressively advance on a working fire. Since the rescue squad is often more experienced, they may help, or take over, the interior attack in order to be more aggressive. The same is true concerning the crew that reports to the roof for ventilation. If the fire occurs in an area where the firefighters do not have a lot of fire duty, perhaps the rescue squad company can do a better or quicker job of ventilating the roof to aid those making the interior attack, who are taking a beating from heavy smoke and hot gases. Viewed by some as overbearing or self-centered, the rescue squad members are not immune from personality conflicts with other firefighters who are able to perform the same duties with equal precision.

Squad companies receive additional training and will usually be members of special teams. Water recovery or scuba diving, high-angle rescue or rappelling, below-grade, confined-space, or trench rescue, and haz mat (hazardous materials) teams train for situations requiring added expertise and equipment knowledge. Since this equipment is part of the rescue squad's complement of tools, they must know how to use them all.

Members of FDNY Rescue 2 assemble ropes and other rigging supplies to carry into the building where a scaffold collapsed. One woman died as a result of the collapse, which forced city officials to close several square blocks of Times Square.

is still in the harness on the firefighter's back or when the air bottle is loose. Loud bells serve as alarms telling firefighters that their air bottle needs to be refilled. The filling process takes approximately 2 minutes and will be performed by the operator of the air or rescue unit. The SCBA industry has produced two different styles. High- and low-pressure systems each require different methods for filling bottles, and not all cascade setups can accommodate both types.

Occasionally, a rescue squad will be designed with a small water tank and fire pump allowing it to increase the types of calls it can handle, although this is not the norm.

The tools themselves are designed for different applications. Some examples include a porta-power, which is a manually operated hydraulic spreader, and a come-along, which is a hand winch. Cribbing, or blocks of wood, is used to secure an auto that is in an unstable position. When the vehicle is lifted during a rescue, the cribbing is inserted underneath to stabilize the vehicle and hold it in place. Cribbing is also used to secure an area that may collapse, like a ditch or hole in the ground endangering a victim or the rescuers. Made of hardwoods, cribbing consists of different lengths of 4x4s, or specially formed shapes that are tied together forming steps for securing irregular objects.

Ropes have many uses in rescue work. Aside from being essential for rappelling and handling rescues down a hill or on the outside of a high-rise building, ropes are used as safety lines for victims, rescuers, and equipment. Unlike several years ago when all rope was made of hemp, rescue ropes are now made of special blends to prevent kinking, unraveling, and fraying.

Air bags are made of heavy rubber, or Kevlar, and can be inflated to lift heavy loads. One use involves lifting a car that has flipped onto its roof, providing room for the rescuers to crawl underneath and remove the victim. Air bags are inserted flat and then inflated with air using a compressor and a regulator.

They can also be inflated with SCBA bottles. Once inflated, they can support a tremendous amount of weight. When the rescue is completed, the air is slowly released, lowering the car or other obstacle back to the ground safely. Different shapes, sizes, and lifting capacities make up the complement of air bags carried.

Resembling the jaws and teeth of an alligator, hydraulic extrication tools are commonly referred to as "the Jaws of Life." Several companies manufacture similar tools, each with a multitude of attachments and refinements to handle distinct jobs. These tools can be powered by gas or electric generators. Often, a rescue squad will carry several types of tools and power supplies. If the rescue squad can position itself close enough to the scene, they will use a truck-mounted generator with a tool attached to long cord reels that are ready to use immediately. Scenes that are farther away will necessitate a portable generator with the tools carried to the site. Some rescue squads will have tools mounted on either side of the truck to facilitate access depending on the truck's proximity to the rescue.

Accessories for the jaws include rams, cutters, and spreaders. Rams are used to force something open, or as braces put in between two objects to keep

Firefighters repack their tools on a specially designed roll-out shelf after completing a rescue.

Firefighters line up to have their SCBA bottles topped off at the scene of a fire.

incident with their own refined protocol. Although tasks are similar, variations occur depending on the actual incident.

Structure fires, for example, present different challenges to responding fire companies. As the rescue squad responds, the company officer will listen to the radio chatter between the first-arriving companies and the chief officer to determine where their resources may be needed. The officer is constantly considering what he has on board that no one else does that would be useful at the scene. Paying close attention to the size-up given by the first-arriving companies helps to determine just what tools are needed. The driver will position the apparatus close to the fire building so that they have access to retrieve more of their equipment if needed. At the same time, the rescue squad must stay out of the way of engine and truck companies, which need to place their rigs closer to the fire building. Another consideration for the rescue squad is that they may leave the scene to respond elsewhere before all of the other units leave. This means it is important for them not to be boxed in.

At a commercial fire in a store front, the rescue squad will arrive on the scene and report to the front of the building to assist with making entry. If the first companies have trouble gaining access into the building, the rescue squad will have metal cutting saws, torches, and heavy tools to break in. If entry has been made, the rescue squad will leave their tools on the sidewalk, or by another rig, and help the companies fighting the fire. The rescue squad may be responsible for taking a second line into the building.

A high-rise fire brings other considerations. Again, the vehicle has little bearing on which functions the company members will perform. With an average crew of six, each firefighter will most likely report to the building carrying a spare air bottle. Together, they will also bring ropes for search and rescue, pike poles for pulling ceilings, and axes and battering rams for forcing doors. Their assignment will take them to the floor above the fire to search

them from moving. Cutters are giant scissors used most often to cut the posts around the windshield that support the roof of a car. After the windshield is removed and the posts are cut, the roof of the vehicle can be raised, creating a convertible where there once was a sedan. Spreaders are used to create an open area where something has collapsed or is crushed. In the closed position, the spreaders are pushed into a tight spot and then, as they expand, the two objects that had been forced together will separate. Spreaders, cutters, and rams come in different sizes and shapes to handle many different situations.

Duties

Each rescue squad will have its own set of general working orders and procedures. Not to say that they do different things, but they may approach each

This rare scene is the result of a major construction accident involving 26 floors of scaffolding in Manhattan. Four of the five FDNY rescue companies were on the scene together.

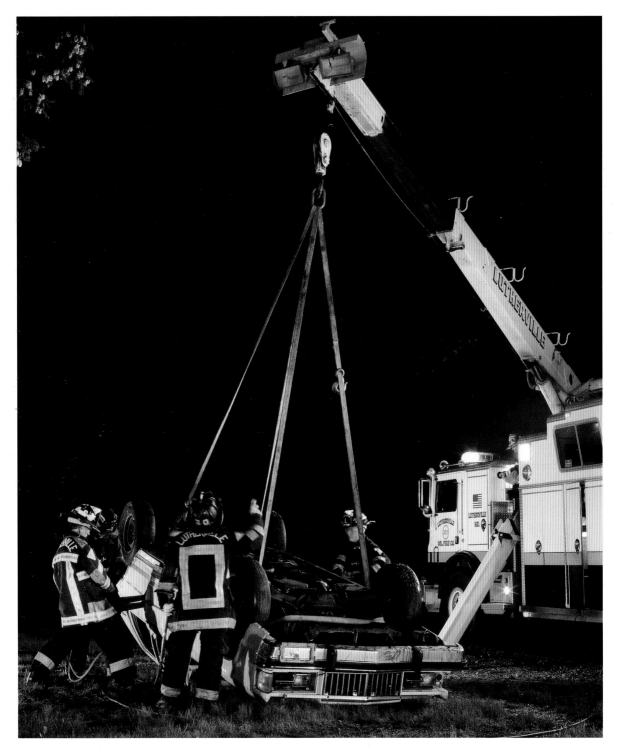

for and rescue building occupants. Any doors that are closed will be forced open to make sure no one is trapped. After completing this task, they will leave their tools and assist other companies that are attacking the fire. Ropes are used to provide an escape route in the event the floor becomes untenable and the firefighter has to retreat in poor conditions, or if the firefighter becomes disoriented or lost. If someone is manning a handline, the hose provides the escape path to follow.

Single- and multiple-family residential fires, where the buildings are close together, are handled differently from commercial and high-rise fires. Whether the structure is called a row house, walk-up, brownstone, or bungalow, the approach for the rescue squad is the same. Again, approaching with six firefighters, the company will separate into three crews of two firefighters each and split as follows: two to the roof, two to the front door, and two to the rear. The roof crew will climb an aerial and follow the truck company with saws and axes to assist with ventilation. There are never too many saws on the scene. If the attack is being made from the front, the front door squad crew will report with forcible-entry tools and pike poles. They will attempt to gain access to the floor above the fire for search and rescue. The rear company will do the same if they have better access, otherwise either company will assist with the handlines working at the seat of the fire.

Accident scenes present still other considerations for the rescue squad. Here again, the driver wants to position his apparatus as close to the incident as possible for ease of access to the equipment on board. This is not always possible because other companies or the police department may have arrived earlier. Again, listening to the size-up from the companies on the scene will determine just what

Lutherville, Maryland, operates this unique rescue squad, which has a crane to assist with many types of rescues. Here, the crane secures an overturned auto as the crew uses hydraulic tools to open the vehicle.

tools are needed right away. The rescue squad will assist the preliminary companies and take over the rescue only if the others are not able to complete the rescue or if the incident commander requests they do so. Like any job, working with other people and knowing how to interact goes a long way toward achieving the common goal of facilitating a safe and expedient rescue.

Since EMS responses are numerous for every fire department, a rescue squad may be dispatched to assist with medical emergencies. Although the rare rescue squad will have the capability to transport a patient to a hospital, most will have BLS or ALS medical capabilities. A recent trend is to build storage for medical equipment and supplies into the crew area of the cab. This makes access to these items very easy for the firefighters.

Salvage duties may be part of a rescue squad's responsibilities for suburban departments, but not generally in the larger cities. Salvage involves trying to reduce water damage to personal property, and the subsequent cleanup. This requires vacuums capable of picking up standing water, squeegees, brooms, and shovels to assist homeowners and business owners with cleanup from the water used to douse the fire. Big cities will generally leave these duties to private contractors who are all too eager to help for a fee.

In the last decade, incidents involving chemicals and poisons have grown substantially. Referred to as hazardous materials or haz mats, health and safety concerns for firefighters have steadily increased. Whereas a fire department might have carried a single, disposable, protective suit and some gloves in the past, now the amounts of supplies necessary to satisfy OSHA and EPA requirements are enormous. More often than not, special units designated to handle haz mat situations will respond to these incidents. The rescue squad will work with the haz mat unit and will also carry haz mat supplies. Detection meters and protective suits are part of the equipment that will help the rescue squad when they arrive at a haz mat situation.

The most common duties for a rescue squad involve . . . rescues. The term *rescue* encompasses many different situations, including accidents with industrial machines, scaffolding, and anything that can trap someone. Numerous types of construction accidents occur involving falls, collapses, and workers stranded in precarious places. By far, the greatest number of responses for most rescue squads involve motor vehicle accidents where the occupant is trapped or pinned in the vehicle. Although most of these incidents are not serious and the rescue can be performed with a pry bar before the rescue squad arrives, the ever-increasing severity of accidents on our nation's roads provides new challenges daily for these highly trained professionals. Whether the vehicle is demolished, rolled over, stuck under a tractor-trailer, in a body of water, or down an embankment, the process of removing the trapped occupants is called extrication.

When the report comes in that a traffic accident has occurred and there may be entrapment, a rescue squad will be dispatched to the scene. Often, the first-arriving company will be an engine or medic unit, who will do the size-up to determine if they can handle the incident or if the rescue squad is needed. The rescue squad carries a vast array of tools to handle any job they may encounter. Certain rescue squads also have incorporated a crane mounted to the truck's frame to assist with heavy lifting. Others are equipped for all manner of trench, cave-in, or water rescues.

Rescue squads are considered by some to be the elite of the department and to have one of the most exciting jobs. In reality, they work alongside the engine and truck companies as an equal partner on the team.

Three engine companies assist a rescue squad removing the trapped victims of an auto accident. In order to gain access to the victim, the car's roof was cut at the front posts and opened like a convertible.

CHAPTER 5

SPECIAL UNITS

Workers didn't need to be told what the creaking noises meant as they ascended the construction elevator outside the 26-story building in Times Square. They quickly shouted over their radios that the scaffold was about to come down, alerting pedestrians and co-workers alike to get clear. Moments later with a loud crushing sound, 14 floors of steel dropped the equivalent of one story to rest on the bottom 10 floors. One of the two elevator tracks came raining down on a neighboring building and the street below. The incident would turn out to require a fire department presence for several days. The Mobile Command Post was ordered to the scene as a base for chiefs and other supervisory personnel.

FDNY's Mobile Command Post responds to prolonged incidents. Seen here in Manhattan, the unit provides a controlled environment for monitoring the scene. It is also equipped with a light tower and video camera on the roof.

Many departments supplement their fleets with specialized rigs to handle unique situations and hazards that face emergency professionals every day. Units are built for foam applications, removal of high volumes of smoke, cave-ins, hazardous materials, high-angle rescues, swift water rescues, nighttime lighting, communications and command, and the delivery of massive amounts of water. Often it is the luxury of large departments to be able to enhance their fleets with specialized equipment that may rarely be called into service. Smaller departments share these resources with surrounding departments to offset the cost, training, and maintenance that are involved, or they will utilize other apparatus to perform these tasks to the best of their abilities.

Communications and Command

Communication units are among the most common single-function special units. Many of these are converted buses, vans, or delivery trucks. They consist of banks of radios with positions for operators to sit while controlling the communications and record keeping at a scene. The seats inside the vehicle provide protection from the outside elements and minimize distractions while keeping the personnel close to the incident commanders.

These vehicles can also be used as a command post for the chiefs in order to keep track of the companies working at the scene. Whether the incident is a fire, major motor vehicle accident, or a disaster, the inside command post allows the chiefs to

Chicago operates four mobile communications units throughout the city. Unit 2-7-2 is shown at the scene of an apartment fire. Chiefs and support personnel are able to monitor the scene from within a climate-controlled environment.

work in a controlled environment. Some chiefs prefer to direct the scene from an outside position that is either fixed or allows them to move around the scene. In this case, they will delegate others to the command vehicle to keep track of the orders that the commander issues.

Most communication and command vehicles have windows allowing the workers who are inside to see the incident. These units usually respond with one person who serves as the driver and primary radio operator. When the driver arrives on the scene, the unit is positioned as close to the incident as possible without getting in the way of the companies that are working. Once on the scene, protocol will dictate who is assigned to work in the comm-van. The preplanned running cards, which outline what equipment is due to respond to each type of incident, will dictate when the comm-van is dispatched.

Deluge Wagons

When an attack on a fire turns defensive, many situations require the delivery of huge amounts of water for a prolonged period to extinguish the fire and smoldering remains. Generally, this is accomplished by using master streams from engines and aerials in addition to portable master streams at street level. Occasionally, a department has at its disposal a rig designed as an enormous deluge gun. This truck will have multiple large-diameter inlets to accommodate various engines pumping water through one or more super deluge guns. As a reference point, the standard diameter of a deck-mounted deluge gun on a pumper is 1 3/8 inches. These massive rigs will have guns with diameters up to 2 1/4 inches, which provide a tremendous system for high-volume water delivery.

Below-Grade Rescue

Special rescue applications have created the need to store and transport large amounts of equipment for cave-ins (also known as below-grade rescues) and confined-space rescues. Below-grade rescues are most

The FDNY Field Communications Unit works at a scene in Manhattan.

often the result of construction work. As large trenches, ditches, and holes are dug, the contractor will usually lower a steel cage into the opening to protect the workers in case the sides give way. Sometimes this is done with heavy wooden timbers or steel beams.

In the event that a breach occurs trapping a worker or workers, the below-grade rescue team is called. Arriving after the first-due engine and truck companies, the special team comes with hand tools, rigging, braces, support jacks, and large amounts of lumber for shoring up the work area. In order to protect the rescue workers and the victims, workers will dig and add braces as they go. Sheets of plywood, 2x and 4x lumber stock along with hydraulic tools are used together to hold back the walls of a trench or other work area that is below the grade level of the surrounding area.

When the below-grade team arrives, they become the primary crew working at the scene. The engine and truck companies work to support the efforts of the special team.

If the work area is completely underground, the challenges greatly increase. Fewer people can work in the confined spaces and there is considerably less room to maneuver. The crews need to have many

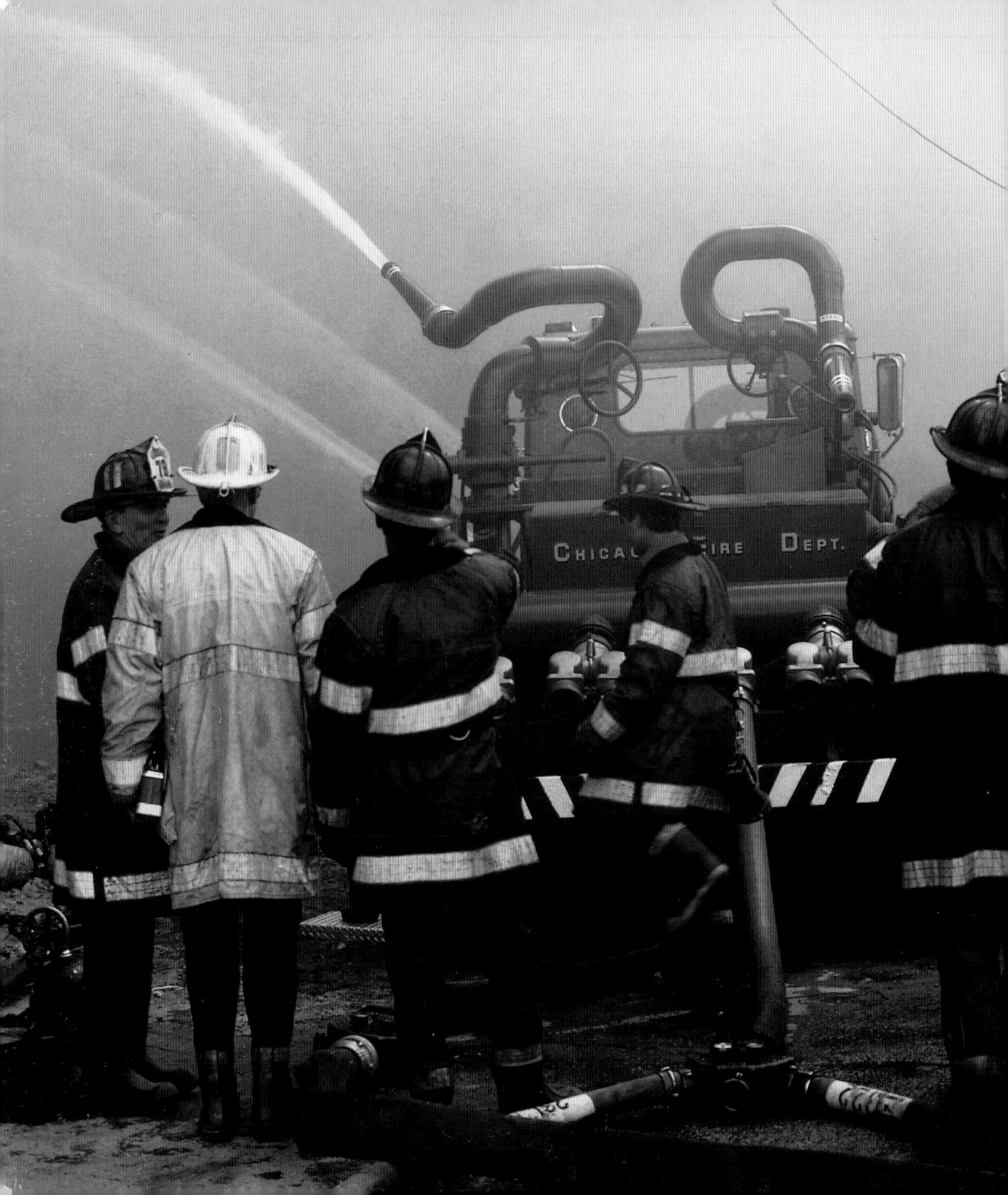
FIRE DEPT.

specialized tools and support equipment to properly perform the rescue. Much of the same equipment is shared with the below-grade rescues, and therefore the specialized rigs can serve both functions.

High-Angle Rescue

Another specialized area of training within the fire service deals with victims who become trapped high above the ground. Whether it is a construction worker tangled in rigging or a window washer stuck on a scaffold, the high-angle recovery team is called to perform the rescue. These are firefighters who have been trained in rappelling and rope work to lower themselves to the victim, release the victim, and safely get him or her to the ground, roof, or other safe vantage point. Municipal water towers provide a unique location for a rescue and often serve as the training ground for these teams. Often, this team incorporates their equipment and supplies into a rescue squad. Otherwise, they have their own vehicle outfitted with ropes, harnesses, helmets, and other items necessary to perform their tasks.

Hazardous Materials Units

Over the last decade or so, there has been an increase in fire loads containing hazardous chemicals and poisonous gases. The fire service has become increasingly more responsive to these dangers in

Below-grade team members use wood and support jacks to reinforce the trenches at the site of a cave-in.

One of the CFD's deluge units works at an extra-alarm fire. Note that the unit has a far greater capacity than what is being utilized at this scene.

Below-grade rescues require a large amount of lumber to reinforce the area near a trapped victim. Firefighters are unloading sheets of plywood for the shoring up process.

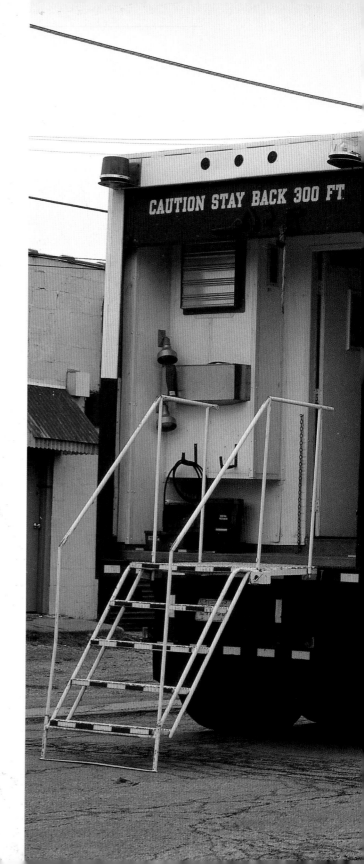

terms of protecting the environment and providing for the safety of firefighters. In doing so, fire departments have expanded their response capabilities to handle these situations. Hazardous materials response units have emerged from a simple extension of the rescue squad to an entire specialization of manpower, equipment, and supplies. While most rescue squads carry various detection meters, some protective suits, and other basic supplies to handle hazardous materials calls as first responders, anything that poses serious dangers will require a response from the haz mat teams.

Apart from large cities that can dedicate around-the-clock personnel to the haz mat team, other teams will consist of members, referred to as technicians, from many departments, who respond to the incident and assemble into teams on the scene.

Haz mat units range from small vans to the large squad-type apparatus with supplemental support vehicles carrying supplies, decontamination facilities, computers, faxes, libraries, and mobile command posts. One popular style of vehicle is the

This tractor-trailer combination provides an area for the decontamination of the entry team at a haz mat incident.

M.A.B.A.S.
DIV
WILL CO.
KANE CO.
M.A.B.A.S.
DIV. 10
COOK CO.
DUPAGE CO.
THANKS TO OUR SPONSORS
Mobile
Decontamination
Generator

A converted beverage delivery truck serves this haz mat team well by carrying a tremendous amount of equipment and supplies.

beverage delivery truck with roll up doors that has been converted to a haz mat unit capable of carrying large quantities of supplies. Although most departments would like to design and order specialized apparatus for their own purposes, many rely on vehicle donations from corporations or industrial complexes in their districts. It is for the good of the department, the local industry, and the community to see that the haz mat team is properly equipped for response to these emergencies.

Different levels of protective suits are included in the haz mat team's supplies. Depending on the degree of corrosiveness of the hazardous product, suits offer various levels of protection for the firefighters. Portable showers and tubs are carried to provide decontamination for personnel who make entry into the hot zone where the dangers are greatest. Several sizes and types of containers are carried to hold products that have been spilled and need to be contained

for proper disposal. Specialized meters, absorbent materials for soaking up spilled liquids, and diking material to prevent a hazardous liquid from running free to contaminate water supplies and sewers are among the supplies carried by a haz mat team.

Haz mat operations are not quick. Caution is exercised in every aspect of a haz mat incident to ensure safety.

Light Wagons

Most engines and trucks carry auxiliary lighting to assist with nighttime emergencies. The majority of these units have 500-watt quartz lights mounted to poles that telescope up, rotate, and swivel to add illumination to the scene. Rescue squads will generally be able to supplement the lighting of the engines and trucks with more lights powered by a larger generator.

Additional units whose sole purpose is to provide huge amounts of light covering a broad area are not uncommon. These light units consist of a large generator, telescoping quartz lights, portable lights that are removable, and one or more big towers with multiple lights. Again, the light wagon may be the rescue squad or a unit dedicated solely to lighting.

Several companies manufacture towers, which can range from 2,000 watts to 6,000 watts with the ability to extend 42 feet above the truck. To get an appreciation for the amount of lighting that is possible for one truck to produce, imagine an entire football field illuminated from a vehicle parked at the 50-yard line pointing a tower toward each end zone.

Not all fire departments use supplemental lighting at fire scenes. It is a luxury that is not available to every department. In today's environment of stretching budget dollars and trying to maximize the potential of every unit, many departments have added auxiliary light towers onto the roof of the engine's cab. Since the engine is placed close to the scene, it is in an ideal location to provide lighting for the scene. In some cases, a pumper will have two independent towers mounted on the cab roof. Each tower has its own remote control to raise and lower the unit, and direct the lights where they can do the most good.

Foam Units

Chemical fires are extinguished using foam instead of water. Many engines are equipped with built-in foam systems that enable immediate access to foam for these applications. Foam concentrate is stored in a tank and can be mixed with water on demand to produce the proper foam mixture for fighting these special fires. Other engines carry foam concentrate in cans and an adapter called an eductor.

Haz mat techs in entry suits prepare to enter into the hot zone at an incident.

FDNY Tac 2 lights up the scene after a scaffold collapse in Manhattan. In the background, some of the construction debris can be seen lying across the street.

The eductor taps into the can, mixing the foam concentrate with water to produce the proper consistency.

In certain environments to which large municipal and industrial departments respond, it is not uncommon to find units that are specifically designed as foam pumpers. These units will have considerably larger foam tanks and, often, large deck guns for application of the foam product. Gasoline tanker truck fires, petroleum storage containers in tank farms, electrical plants, refineries, and aircraft emergencies are the prime areas of use for foam units.

Swift Water Rescue

Rivers, streams, and man-made channels for water runoff can turn deadly in a matter of minutes when severe storms bring large amounts of water in a short period of time. As the water level rises, the speed of the current increases rapidly and can sweep people off their feet or an entire car from the road. When this occurs, it becomes dangerous for the rescuers as well as the victims. Called swift water rescue, this type of incident has brought about the need for specialized training and equipment to ensure everyone's safety. These vehicles carry ropes, life vests, helmets, and several firefighters to an incident.

Smoke Ejectors

A smoke ejector is a fan. In addition to natural ventilation, which comes from windows, doors, and holes in the roof, a smoke ejector also clears smoke from a building. The City of Chicago Fire Department

A Civil Defense light unit illuminates the scene of an extra-alarm fire.

Philadelphia's air unit responds to working jobs to refill SCBA bottles. This unit also carries many spare bottles that are ready to be used.

carries two special vehicles on its roster, which are both smoke ejectors. Originally built in 1961 and rechassied in 1975, the units themselves consist of enormous fans that are PTO-driven. They carry as much as 100 feet of 24-inch-diameter hose. The hose attaches to the fans to pull the smoke out of the building. These units do not see much regular action and are primarily designed to assist with large basement and cellar fires where windows and other conventional ventilation are not available.

Pod Units

As a cost-saving measure and to improve efficiency, several departments have designed pods, which are large steel boxes similar to overseas shipping containers, to store various specialized equipment. These pods are outfitted for specific tasks and are transported via a truck that can hoist them up and roll them off at the scene of an emergency. Similar in delivery to large construction dumpsters, one truck and driver can serve to accommodate several

different special teams with their equipment. The driver can deposit the pod and leave to retrieve another, or return to service ready to assist other teams with their specialized pods.

Canteens

Another piece of apparatus that is often at the scene of large fires or prolonged emergencies is not operated *by* the fire service, but *for* the fire service. The canteen provides food, coffee, hot chocolate, and cold drinks to anyone in need at these scenes, including displaced occupants. Run by the Salvation Army, the Red Cross, volunteer groups, and fire department auxiliary organizations, the canteens fill a void that is welcomed by everyone.

Forest Fire Units

Other specialized units include vehicles involved with the fighting of wildland and forest fires. Bulldozers and flatbed trucks for transport, special four-wheel-drive units for off-road access, army surplus units, and more are all called into action during the dreaded forest fire seasons around the country.

It can probably be said that for each of the specialized units mentioned here, there are others that have been overlooked. Many departments customize units to fill very specific niches, that they encounter which differ from other areas. In the northern and eastern regions of the United States, ice, snow, and severe cold present situations that are unheard of in the south and west. Likewise, earthquakes and seasonal factors present unique requirements along the West Coast that may seem foreign to departments in the Midwest. What every department does have in common, though, is the need to ensure the protection of lives and property in their districts with whatever means they have available.

One of Chicago's smoke ejector units stands ready to assist with a basement fire that escalated to a 5-11 alarm.

CHAPTER 6
AIRPORT FIRE FIGHTING

*A*fter the pilot radioed the control tower that he suspected a problem landing, the airport fire department deployed the ARFF units to predetermined points around the runway. When the plane landed, a firefighter in a protective suit pulled the handline as the driver used the roof and bumper turrets to discharge agent toward the aircraft, safeguarding the passengers and crew.

The Fort Worth, Texas, Fire Department operates a 4x4, E-One Titan ARFF unit. The driver operates the bumper and roof turrets while the firefighter manages the handline.

Extinguishing agent is discharged through the roof turret of an Oshkosh T-3000 ARFF to hit a fire during a training exercise.

Airport fire apparatus is extremely specialized due to the unique threats and potential for injury at an airport. Aircraft emergencies, large quantities of highly flammable liquids, and the vast number of people who work at and pass through airports present risks that can surpass the dangers in many large cities. As a matter of fact, during peak travel times the busiest airports rival some cities in size and population. Calls for emergency medical service, structure fires, and hazardous materials incidents add to aircraft emergencies keeping airport rescue personnel occupied.

Airports are regulated by the Federal Aviation Administration (FAA), which provides regulations that cover such items as signage, lighting, clear zones

Training for airport fire personnel includes working in a simulator. This exercise prepares firefighters for entering a burning aircraft.

for approach and departure areas, widths of the runways, emergency master plans, wildlife hazards, firefighting equipment, and firefighting extinguishing agents. Most commercial airports are assigned an index rating from A (the smallest) through E (the largest), which establishes guidelines for the fire department. The rating is determined by the length of the longest airplane that uses the airport, and the average daily departures for this type of aircraft. The largest aircraft with five or more average daily departures at an airport becomes the benchmark for that airport's index rating. Some airports, served by commercial passenger carriers that fall under the minimum usage and size guidelines, are non-indexed airports and do not need airport rescue firefighting vehicles (ARFF) on site, or as part of the local servicing fire department.

Associated with each index rating are response conditions, which the fire department must meet. These demand that at least one of the vehicles which

After a small military jet crashed onto a residential street, ARFF equipment responded from the air base where the flight originated.

is required by the index minimum can reach the midpoint of the farthest runway in three minutes or less to discharge an agent. The balance of the department's required agent needs to arrive at the same point in under 4 minutes from the time of the alarm.

To extinguish a fire, each vehicle carries water, foam, Halon gas, or dry chemicals, which are referred to as the extinguishing agents, or simply agents. Each agent has special properties and specific uses. Water is used on structure fires and for mixing foam. Foam, otherwise known as aqueous film forming foam (AFFF), is a concentrate that is generally used in a 3-percent mixture with water. It is used for all aircraft applications and fuel fires. Halon, which is a predecessor to its environmentally friendly replacement Halotron, is stored as a liquid but discharges as a gas. It is used in a confined space on electrical fires such as engines or computers. Dry chemical agents, which are either sodium- or potassium-based, are used for wheel fires, running fuel fires, or force-fed fires (fires that are continuously fed by a fuel which is under pressure). Metl-x is for class D metal fires and is stored in fire extinguishers.

Each airport fire department creates guidelines for the type and frequency of training for all person-

nel. Additionally, the department must provide a sufficient-size force to operate the vehicles, meet the response times, and discharge the minimum amount of agent called for by the index rating.

Individual airports have some flexibility when determining their own format for achieving the minimum agent requirements. The guidelines call for a minimum number of vehicles but do not specify the size of each. For instance, the agent guidelines at an airport with an index E call for 6,000 gallons of water to be carried for foam production. The airport can purchase two vehicles with 3,000-gallon capacities or four units each capable of carrying 1,500 gallons.

Most major airports will have two to three times the minimum agent requirement of the FAA due to the size of the airport and the number of runways. The layout and overall size prohibit the fire department from accessing each runway and all other aircraft movement areas in under 3 minutes unless they have multiple fire stations. Each department will determine the number of personnel, fire stations, and ARFF vehicles necessary to properly protect the airport and satisfy the FAA.

Political awareness and correctness have dictated certain changes in airport firefighting terminology. Several years ago, it was determined that the word *crash* had negative connotations to the traveling public. At the time, many airports referred to their stations as crash houses, and the vehicles were crash rescue vehicles (CRVs), or crash trucks. The current phraseology has replaced the word *crash* with *rescue*. Hence, stations are now called rescue houses and the vehicles are airport rescue firefighting vehicles (ARFFs). (Everyone feels safer now.)

Whatever they're called, these vehicles are enormous, all-wheel-drive units that are available as 4x4s, 6x6s, and 8x8s. They are off-road, all-terrain units, generally with independent suspension and special body designs to accommodate steep inclines. Older designs were constructed with two Detroit Diesel engines. One engine would power the vehicle while the other handled pumping. Today, most units have one turbo-charged, Detroit Diesel, V-8 engine with over 600 horsepower.

The FAA requires the largest units with 3,000-gallon capacities to be capable of achieving 0–50 miles per hour in 45 seconds or less. Smaller 1,500 gallon-units need to do the same in 30 seconds, while Rapid Intervention Vehicles, also known as Quick Rescue Vehicles, must accelerate from 0 to 50 miles per hour in 25 seconds or less. All ARFFs must be able to travel at 60 miles per hour.

ARFFs carry water and foam. Halon and dry chemicals may be carried on the same units or on other vehicles that do not have water and foam. These units will have roof-mounted turrets and most also have a turret mounted on the front bumper. Each ARFF has at least one handline for each agent carried. The fire pumps are generally 1,500- or 1,750-gallon-per-minute capacities. Again, the government has guidelines for this depending on the size of the water tank and required discharge rates from the roof turret. All ARFFs have pump-and-roll capabilities, which means they can pump water or foam while the vehicle is moving.

ARFFs today also have nozzles under the truck in the event that fire gets under the vehicle. The operator can discharge water or foam via the under-truck nozzles to protect the vehicle and occupants. Seating capacity is for three or four firefighters. ARFFs at civilian airports generally have a crew of one or two. The driver operates the turrets and the other person will maneuver the handline. In contrast, the Air Force staffs ARFFs

Four people aboard a helicopter were killed when they crashed into the garage of a suburban house. A T-3000 Oshkosh ARFF from O'Hare International Airport responded to the scene to lend assistance.

The pilot of a British Vulcan Bomber with flight control problems avoided a busy highway and ditched his plane into a landfill near a U.S. air base they were visiting. Various Oshkosh ARFF equipment responded along with tankers to extinguish the fires. Unfortunately, the entire crew was unable to eject safely.

heat-seeking cameras, and forward-looking radar with infrared cameras have become standard issue.

Since all aircraft are monitored by the control tower using radar, the tower is able to direct rescue crews to the scene by matching the ARFF's position with that of the aircraft when a mishap occurs on the field in bad weather. The heat-seeking cameras assist with locating victims who are not on an aircraft during an emergency.

Duties

Aside from the duties that airport firefighters share with city and suburban firefighters, the main aspect of their job lies in preparedness for aircraft emergencies. Each airport will determine their own SOPs for different scenarios. Basic responses for aircraft reporting difficulties en route to the airport call for the fire department to deploy their units in thirds. Split evenly between each end of the runway and the midpoint, the crew will await the plane's arrival.

In the event of a safe landing, most units will return to their stations and the incident commander will assign the other units to follow the aircraft to the gate. If the plane lands and has a problem, the pilot will steer the plane off the runway and come to a stop. The fire department will deploy the ARFF units on all sides of the plane and an officer will plug into the plane's intercom system to speak to the flight deck. Generally, it is just a matter of informing the pilot whether there is a fire and to discuss the need to evacuate the plane before it arrives at the gate. If the fire department is not able to speak directly with the pilot via the intercom, they will go through the tower to establish communications. Often something relatively minor will be handled here, allowing the plane to continue on to the gate to release the passengers. The fire department and airline always consider the safety of the occupants first. It is not always necessary to evacuate a plane; in fact, it is preferable to tow the plane to the gate with the passengers and crew on board if possible. Incidents like a blown tire or gear collapse, which damage the aircraft but pose no life

with a crew of four: driver, turret operator, handline, and crew chief.

An interesting aspect to ARFF designs is called central tire inflation/deflation. This allows the driver to let the air out of the tires in the event the unit gets stuck. When the unit is free, the tires can be reinflated with a switch.

Airports cover vast amounts of land and may seem easy to navigate, but the diversity of the roads, runways, and taxiways can create major confusion. Anytime vehicles drive where aircraft also travel, they must be in contact with the control tower. At times, heavy rain, snow, or fog can reduce visibility. It is for this reason that ARFFs are equipped with several items to help them find field emergencies and avoid collisions. Global positioning systems, threat to the passengers, will result in a slow, orderly, safe evacuation on the field using mobile stairway units and buses. Anytime the passengers are evacuated via the emergency slides, 10–20 percent of the occupants will go to the hospital for minor injuries dealing with ankles, knees, backs, and elbows.

In the event of an engine fire, one of two scenarios may take place. First, if there is no threat to the occupants of the plane, the fire department will pull a handline and extinguish the fire with Halon to save the engine. The Halon will prevent further damage to the engine and save the airline from unnecessary expenses and repairs. If the fire is impinging on the fuselage and endangering the occupants, foam will be used to douse the fire.

An interior fire in the cabin will result in the ARFFs surrounding the aircraft in a standby mode, while the cabin crew determines the path for the evacuation. The engine, truck, and squad companies, or the public safety officers, will assist with the evacuations when the slides deploy. Fire crews will enter the cabin after the evacuation by climbing the slides, placing small ladders to the doorways, or by laddering the wing to get lines on the fire. The FAA mandates that a full aircraft must be able to be evacuated in 90 seconds or less using half of the exits. Airport fire personnel say that actual emergencies live up to this mandate.

Upon arriving at an aircraft incident or crash with a fire, the ARFF personnel's primary goal is to separate the fire from the fuselage. If this is not possible, then it is imperative to cut and maintain a rescue path for the passengers and crew. If a path exists, the survivors will find it.

Although some of the busiest civilian airports in the United States average three ARFF standbys a day, the majority never amount to anything and the traveling public does not even know they occurred. Fortunately, most incidents that do require action by ARFFs are relatively minor fires in the wheel assemblies or the engines and do not pose a threat to the safety of the passengers. Occasionally, a hard landing will result in damage to the landing gear assembly requiring the plane to be towed to the gate or evacuated on the field. In any case, highly trained personnel with specialized equipment stand ready in the unlikely event that an air carrier requires their services.

INDEX